Second Marriage

Also by Richard B. Stuart

ACT THIN: STAY THIN

HELPING COUPLES CHANGE

SLIM CHANCE IN A FAT WORLD

TRICK OR TREATMENT

Second Marriage

Make it happy!
Make it last!

Richard B. Stuart
and
Barbara Jacobson

W·W·Norton & Company
New York   London

Published simultaneously in Canada by Penguin Books Canada Ltd,
2801 John Street, Markham, Ontario L3R 1B4.
Printed in the United States of America.

The text of this book is composed in Times Roman,
with display type set in Tiffany.
Composition and manufacturing by The Haddon Craftsmen, Inc.
Book design by Jacques Chazaud

First Edition

Library of Congress Cataloging in Publication Data

Stuart, Richard B.
Second Marriage.

Bibliography: p.
Includes index.
1. Remarriage. I. Jacobson, Barbara. II. Title.
HQ1018.S78   1985   306.8′4   84–29441

ISBN 0-393-01910-1

W. W. Norton & Company, Inc.
500 Fifth Avenue, New York, N. Y. 10110
W. W. Norton & Company, Ltd.
37 Great Russell Street, London WC1B 3NU

1 2 3 4 5 6 7 8 9 0

For C.H.S.

Contents

Authors' Note

Our book is offered to those who want to do everything possible to make sure their second marriages are happier and more long-lasting than their first. The suggestions offered here are based upon many years of practicing marriage and family therapy, our experience of living through just about all of the challenges of separation and remarriage, and a thorough review of the marriage and family research literature.

Most of this literature is pessimistic: it describes the problems of second marriages in grim detail, offering much sympathy but little help. We agree that it's important to be realistic about the problems that can complicate a second marriage, but it's even more important to learn how to meet these challenges by turning them into opportunities for change and growth.

Because each marriage is unique, no pat formulas can be universally applied. But while the details may differ, remarrying couples must come to grips with many of the same issues. We'll give you a chance to compare your experience with that of other couples, because knowing that certain conflicts are normal can lessen their sting considerably. We will then help you unravel the complexity of the issues that will arise, offering guidelines and exercises for specific actions you can take to meet each challenge.

While there are many books on second marriage, we believe you will find some special things in ours. Because we are very optimistic about chances for happiness in second marriages, we focus on solutions, not problems. Rather than just telling you to avoid the mistakes of a first marriage or burdening you with fears about what you'll find in the second, we make specific suggestions. For example, we'll help you make sense of your first marriage, understand the secret contract you and your new spouse have created, and develop the joy of shared intimacies. We will also help you find practical methods for making decisions about how to handle work, money, and stepchildren. In short, our goal is to help you have fun and grow—both personally and as a couple—as you enjoy the satisfactions your second marriage now offers and build its power to offer more.

We are extremely grateful to Carol Houck Smith, our editor. She shared in the development of the concept of our book, played a very active role in shaping its content and style, and offered her constant support and encouragement during the stages of its creation. We also owe thanks to Vivienne Jacobson, whose critical reading of our manuscript resulted in some of its more pleasing refinements.

Richard B. Stuart
Barbara Jacobson

Salt Lake City, Utah

Second Marriage

1
Success and Failure in Second Marriage

Not very long ago, men and women met, fell in love, married, and stayed together for life. What their marriages may have lacked in satisfaction, they certainly made up for in stability.

Today men and women have "relationships" and marry if they feel the "chemistry is right." They stay together only until one or the other thinks they've found someone better or believes that single life offers more than staying married. While modern couples may have more opportunities for happiness than their parents ever had, their marriages don't begin to have the stability their parents were able to enjoy.

Despite hopes of "happily ever after" at the altar, about half of all of today's first marriages are destined to end in divorce. For a time, the spectre of divorce seemed to deter some people from marrying, and the lure of freedom seemed to induce ever increasing numbers of couples to end their marriages. The statistics were so alarming that many observers wrote off the two-parent family as a vestige of the past.

Lately, though, people have demonstrated their confidence in marriage in the ways that count most: the rate of marriage has been rising, while the divorce rate has begun a slow but steady decline.

Divorce makes sense for some mismatched couples. After failing in honest attempts to make their marriages better, they may have to choose between staying together unhappily or ending their marriage. In the past, all but a nonconforming few suffered through miserable marriages to avoid the stigma of divorce, or to protect their children from life in a broken home. But divorce is now so commonplace that those who don't end a marriage may feel more out of step than those who do. And more people are realizing that children may be better off in single-parent or step families than in their original conflict-ridden homes.

Most people who divorce eventually remarry. Census Bureau reports show that among those 45 or younger, over 80 percent of divorced men and 75 percent of divorced women remarry. Within three to four years, almost every man and woman who wants to tie another knot will find someone with whom to do it.

Strange as it may seem, parents remarry sooner than those without children. It may be that they want and need the extra help in child-rearing, or playing the field may be awkward, difficult, and unappealing for a custodial parent. People with lower incomes marry sooner than those with higher earnings, perhaps because they need a second income to make ends meet. Those who are older or in poor health often have more difficulty finding a new mate, and they may not be able to remarry as quickly as they'd like. But even though it may be difficult to meet that special someone, the desire to do so is almost always powerful enough to provide the motivation to do whatever it takes to find a second spouse.

More than four out of every five men and women who remarry say that their second marriages are happier than their first, according to several studies recently published in the *Journal of Marriage and the Family.* Some couples may tout the joys of their second marriages just because they would be embarrassed to admit to having made a second bad choice. But most seem to have been able to build genuinely more satisfying relationships when they remarried. Yet second marriages are just as likely to end in divorce. Since most of us are happier with our new partners, why aren't the chances of staying married better?

As a start, we should realize that second marriages have a long cast of characters in addition to the husband and wife. Sociologist Jessie Bernard observed that second marriages simply have too many people in them. Everyone who remarries brings friendships that developed during a first marriage. Many also bring children who have long-term ties to the other parent, grandparents, and others. So when we marry for a second time, we often marry a family and not just a mate, and the resulting complications can put a strain on any relationship.

We also bring routines that we developed with first spouses which we expect the second to know and accept. And, of course, we bring memories of former mates. When we are happy with current partners, we think about the failings of the old one; but when we are unhappy, we often idealize the one we left behind. With all of these currents, real and imagined, second marriages are fertile ground for comparisons which, depending on the mood of the day, can make us more or less satisfied with our current situation.

It's also possible that those who turned to divorce as a solution to marital conflict in the past may be likely to do so again. It seems, though, that this is more true for men than women. Men who have divorced once are *slightly more* likely to divorce again, while divorced women are *less* likely to experience a second marital failure.

It can also be argued that those who divorce are less mature emotionally than those who tough it out and stay in unhappy marriages. But it's just as possible that those who leave an unhappy marriage have greater emotional maturity than those who stay because of fear of the uncertainties of divorce.

Having too much or too little money can sometimes jeopardize the chances of success in second marriages. If only one partner brings significant assets, that person may wonder whether it was personal charm or an impressive net worth that led the other to want to marry. And the less affluent partner may feel too much at the mercy of the one who can control the purse strings. If neither brings substantial assets but either or both are supporting children, financial pressures are sure to arise. Whether the stress comes from seeing too little money coming in from former spouses, or too much going out to them, conflict over how to deal with money can pose major challenges for many remarried pairs.

So much for the bad news. The good news is that remarrying couples are older and wiser. As we'll see, age at marriage is a strong predictor of its success. Remarrying couples also have the benefit of having learned what they can contribute to a marriage and what they expect in return. And perhaps most important, they realize that every relationship has lows as well as highs. Success in any marriage depends upon the realization that relationships work because stresses are handled well, not because they are stress-free.

The willingness to change partners rather than behavior when the going gets tough creates a special problem for those entering second marriages. Remarrying partners bring strong convictions about how things are (and are not) to be done, based on the frustrations of their first marriages. Of course, this makes negotiation difficult. But the challenge is compounded by all the complex interpersonal and financial issues in remarriages. Together, these forces often make the first year of second marriages as trying as the months that set the stage for the first divorce. The failure to put this predictable stress in perspective undoubtedly contributes to the vulnerability of many second marriages. Couples who see the first year as a preview of the best that the new marriage has to offer can doom the marriage to failure. Those who are wise enough to regard these difficult months as a normal stage of relationship development earn the chance to overcome the obstacles and enjoy the greater satisfaction of second marriages.

Until now there have been no "maps" to guide us through the often travelled, yet uncharted territory of remarriage. Those who remarried were like explorers in new lands. We made our journeys without the rituals and supports that accompany every other major life transition from birth to death. Fortunately, now we can do a great deal to improve our chances of happiness in our second marriages.

There can't be any pat solutions to the problems that arise in combined families. One reason is that there are so many variations on the second-marriage theme. For example, either husband or wife might have been single, married once, twice, or even more often. Either or both might have children of whom they may, or may not, be the custodial parent. And either or both could have a relationship with a prior spouse that is active or inactive, positive or negative. There are so many configurations of second marriage that it is impossible for any one set of guidelines to cover every situation a remarried couple might face. As a result, every couple must find its own answers. We can offer maps and instruments, but you will have to chart your own course.

First we'll help you tie up the loose ends of your first marriage. You can't offer your present partner a fair deal if you haven't come to terms with your past. The ability to reach a coherent understanding of first marriage mistakes increases your chances of avoiding them in another marriage. Chapter 2 will help you organize your thoughts about your first marriage in the way that best prepares you for a more satisfying relationship with your new partner.

The choice of a second partner is both easier and more difficult than it was the first time. When you choose a second spouse, you have the benefits of age and experience. You know yourself better, and you have some understanding of what didn't work in your first marriage. But you may also be more set in your ways, more defensive, and more cautious than you were the first time you married. In Chapter 3 you will find suggestions for evaluating the wisdom of your second choice.

Many of the disappointments in marriage are the result of secret agreements made during courtship. Without even realizing what you are doing, you and your new mate have already established expectations that will strongly influence your satisfaction with your marriage. The process of developing these "secret contracts" is discussed in Chapter 4, where guidelines are offered for understanding and openly negotiating the terms.

Almost all couples have some disagreements about money, and those in second marriages have more financial concerns than younger couples marrying for the first time. Suggestions for managing finances in second marriages will be presented in Chapter 5. We'll review the advantages and disadvantages of antenuptial agreements, discuss the one-pot and three-pot models of managing money, and outline a process for making decisions about the use of money.

Most people who have gone through a divorce feel their ex-spouses never really understood what made them tick. Chapter 6 will take the mystery out of good communication and offer guidelines for achieving in your second marriage the understanding that was probably lacking in your first.

No marriage is free from conflict, but the way in which conflict is managed has a profound impact on the quality of the relationship. The skills for handling conflict in second marriages will be discussed in Chapter 7, where we'll explain how spouses can learn to understand each other's perspective and resolve disagreements through negotiation rather than coercion.

Many couples have difficulty meeting the demands of their work and giving their marriage the attention it deserves. In Chapter 8, we will describe several ways couples cope with the time crunch that is inevitable when employment demands are added to family needs. We will also offer guidelines for negotiating an equitable division of responsibilities.

Because at least sixty percent of remarrying couples have children from previous marriages, the success of many second marriages hinges on the way the stepparent is integrated into the family. If the children do not live with you, they may visit often and require some financial support. If you do have custody, day-to-day events will present constant challenges. Many children don't know the meaning of closed doors, and demand a tremendous amount of attention. Furthermore, their care is always at least twice as expensive as anyone dreamed possible. As a result, a stepparent's life has a lot in common with a teenager's: it involves trying to catch a few moments of privacy away from family intrusions, feeling pulled in twenty directions at once, and never having enough money.

Delicate relationship problems almost always develop in combined families. As a start, everyone is confused about the role of stepparent, which is still somewhat negative and ill-defined. The stepparent and child who are strangers are expected to form a loving parent-child relationship despite the fact that the child often doesn't need or want another father or mother. They are expected to develop an attachment immediately, despite the fact that neither knows or understands the other's ways. And they are required to respect a host of unspoken rules of loyalty to all the key adults in the child's life. But stepparenting can be a joy to all concerned. The child has an opportunity to have a loving relationship with another adult who can be as much a friend as a parent. And the stepparent can play a satisfying role in the life of a child who is someone new to love.

To help you start to think differently about stepparenting, in Chapter 9 we will describe five of the most common myths about steprelations, and then we'll offer suggestions for meeting many of the challenges that arise in every newly combined family.

Because extramarital sex so often contributes to the ending of a first marriage, the threat of infidelity may hover over second marriages. In Chapter 10, we will discuss the causes and effects of extramarital sex, and we will offer a structure for the discussion of your own definitions and expectations of fidelity.

After all the practical details are worked out, the best way to make a marriage rewarding and stable is by creating and sustaining intimacy. People who were hurt by the ending of a trusted relationship may be reluctant to allow themselves to be vulnerable again. But the benefits of a close and caring relationship are well worth the risks. In Chapter 11, we'll discuss the techniques of establishing the openness and acceptance that give marriage its meaning.

Many of us fall into one of two traps: we lose sight of how much we have, or we ignore problems until they are overwhelming. The inventory on the next page should help you avoid both traps. It will identify areas in which your marriage is trouble-free and potential danger spots. It's always better to greet the devil by name than to pretend he doesn't exist. By anticipating difficulties, you can be in a much stronger position to conquer them.

In response to questions such as these, it is natural, but not useful, to focus only on problems without giving equal weight to areas in which you are both functioning smoothly. Therefore we strongly suggest that you begin the review of your responses to this and every other exercise in the book with a full discussion of areas in which you are both content. After discussing strengths, you will both be more likely to constructively discuss areas in which change would be useful. The identification of difficulties is the first step in working together to overcome them.

You and your partner should read these statements separately and indicate your agreement or disagreement with each before comparing answers.

INVENTORY OF POTENTIAL STRESSES

1. Either my spouse or I spend an uncomfortable amount of time talking or thinking about a former spouse. (Chapter 2)	Yes	No
2. I am even less like my new spouse than like my first. (Chapter 3)	Yes	No
3. So far, the new marriage has not lived up to my expectations. (Chapter 4)	Yes	No
4. We have disagreements about money management. (Chapter 5)	Yes	No
5. At least one of us often feels misunderstood. (Chapter 6)	Yes	No
6. We fight unfairly or too often. (Chapter 7)	Yes	No
7. Either, or both, of us feels overburdened with the demands of home, jobs, children, and marriage. (Chapter 8)	Yes	No
8. At least one of us is a stepparent. (Chapter 9)	Yes	No
9. At least one of us has had an affair in a previous marriage. (Chapter 10)	Yes	No
10. At least one of us feels a lack of intimacy too often for comfort. (Chapter 11)	Yes	No

Most readers will agree with at least half of these statements. That's nothing more than a reminder that couples in second marriages have to clear many hurdles. As you anticipate and accept the challenges, you can learn how to use your resources to meet them successfully. Each "yes" is an indication of a potential stress that you can successfully resolve. The earlier you identify areas where change is needed, the greater the likelihood that your new marriage will offer the happiness you both count on it to deliver.

Everyone who remarries wants the new marriage to be much happier than the last one. While some simply hope for good luck, it's best to give luck a boost by taking steps to increase the chances for a happy marriage. Success is never accidental: coincidence may have helped you meet your partner, but it takes a positive outlook and a lot of effort to create and sustain a good relationship. Here are some of the beliefs and attitudes needed to make a second marriage work:

1. Realistic expectations that every marriage has good and bad times
2. The willingness to examine your role in every positive and negative exchange in your relationship
3. The willingness to consider everything negotiable, with no demands that your partner accept your way of doing things without fair consideration of alternatives
4. The willingness to consistently learn to understand your partner's point of view
5. A commitment to try different ways of doing things long enough to see if the new way works
6. The maturity to forgive your partner for mistakes made in good faith efforts to make your marriage better

We count on you to bring the motivation to make your marriage work. You can count on us to help you understand many of the issues that will arise and to suggest guidelines for successfully meeting these challenges. If you're in a second marriage that could be improved, we'll help you make it better. And if your new marriage already makes you very happy, we'll help you make it great.

2

Unfinished Business: Coming to Terms with First Marriages

*T*he way we try to make sense of our experience during our first marriages has a profound effect on our chances for success in the second. If we try to ignore the past, or don't correctly understand it, we may have to relive past mistakes time and time again. On the other hand, a balanced perspective on even the most dismal experiences in a first marriage can lay the foundation for happiness in the one that follows.

Though you might not want to admit it now, when you met your first spouse, you probably thought you had found the person with whom you would be happy for a lifetime. This hope faded along the way, so when your marriage ended, you were probably left feeling disappointed, guilty, or angry. These feelings can be so overpowering that you might think only about your pain and not about the forces that caused it.

People often make false assumptions when they try to explain what went wrong in their first marriages. Some see themselves as innocent victims of their former spouses' villainy. They don't try to understand their own contributions to the break-up, but instead try to protect themselves with the belief that it was all their partner's fault. Others fatalistically assume that success in marriage is simply a matter of luck. They explain away their problems as genetic mismatch or a quirk of fate, and they hope for a better deal next time. Still others attribute the failure of their marriage to specific forces beyond their control, like an intrusive mother-in-law, a stressful job, or the tiny apartment in which they had too many fights. All three of these orientations—victimization, fatalism, and a projection of responsibility onto outside forces—offer a good measure of self justification. The price of this is a high probability that the mistakes will be made again.

Alan and Martha, now divorced, each felt victimized by the other's infidelity. For the last year of their marriage, they fought over who was the first to begin an affair. Alan felt Martha was too involved in law school to pay enough attention to him, so he started sleeping with a woman he met at work. Martha felt neglected and rejected by Alan, so she started an affair with a man she met in class. No one knows who was the first to have an affair, but their insistence on assigning blame made it impossible for them to try to save the marriage. They ignored the fact that neither gave their marriage the attention it deserved, and they both justified their own affairs as having been reactions to the other's infidelity. The only thing they agreed on was that once the affairs began, both felt so insecure that they invested their energy in their lovers and let their marriage wither. Since both would like to remarry eventually, they can only benefit by understanding the contributions each made to the deterioration of their relationship.

Many of us initially try to accept as little responsibility as possible for the end of our marriage. In a normal attempt to protect and defend ourselves, we prefer to believe we did everything possible to make it work, while our former spouses seemed determined to make it fail. But when we blame others for our past troubles, we can't learn how to improve our lot in the future. We can only hope for better luck or a more cooperative spouse, and we put ourselves at the mercy of forces we can't control.

Although many people accept too little responsibility for the problems in their first marriage, some people accept too much. Some women, in particular, take so much blame for their marital failure that they feel overwhelmed by guilt. Women sometimes equate marital failure with personal failure, and they may doubt their ability to succeed in any marriage. Taking too much responsibility is as unproductive as taking too little. In both cases, we ignore the fact that it takes two people to create a success or failure, with joyful and miserable marriages both being cooperative efforts.

History is apt to repeat itself unless we can understand the way both spouses contributed to everything that happened in the first marriage. We are more likely to avoid the repetition of unhappy experiences if we understand and accept personal responsibility for shaping our own destiny. And we can keep from being paralyzed by guilt if we realize that we do not bear sole responsibility for past problems. This understanding of the dynamics of the past has been called a "sense of coherence." Without it, we may feel victimized by the past and helpless to change the future. With it, we are much better able to visualize and act upon positive plans for change.

Before we can analyze a first marriage, we need to distinguish the problems of the marriage from the stresses of divorce. Divorce leaves almost everyone feeling awful, and in our pain or guilt we tend to distort our memories of the marriage. We can start to put our feelings in perspective by understanding the common reactions to the demise of a marriage.

The Path to Divorce

No two divorces are alike, but most of us experience similar emotions as we travel the path from marriage to divorce. We often start by denying the seriousness of problems. Eventually, the discomfort becomes so extreme that we can no longer deny it, and we may try to discuss and solve the problems we have. When attempts at solutions fail, we usually feel confused, helpless, and then depressed. As depression gives way to anger, we find it easier to begin the process of letting go. And once we become reconciled to the end of the marriage, we may start to work on re-establishing a separate identity.

The decision to divorce may be a relief, but actual separation almost always brings pain. The stress diminishes over time, but there's a lot of suffering along the way. Two factors seem to ease the pain of separation. If the decision was reached gradually, the transition is easier because the extra time gives both partners a chance to adjust. And if the marriage was consistently bad, the escape from ceaseless stress often balances the negative effects of separation.

Researchers have tried to predict who will make the best adjustment to divorce. Some studies show that men have an easier time; others indicate that women do. Mixed results are also found when trying to determine whether initiating the divorce action or keeping custody of the children makes adjustment easier. It seems that our adjustment is predicted not as much by our situation as by our attitudes. We can view separation as a catastrophe from which we will never recover, or we can regard it as an opportunity for change and growth.

We're most likely to meet the challenges of divorce successfully if we don't allow our negative feelings to overwhelm us. The major obstacles to constructive adjustment are the fear and ambivalence we feel after a marriage ends.

No matter how necessary the divorce was, we all have

some fears as we return to single life. We may doubt our ability to manage on our own. We may also worry about whether we will ever find a mate with whom we can be happy. And, at the most basic level, we may be very unsure of our own identity now that we are no longer part of a couple.

Some fears pass as we gradually meet the challenges of life. But we all have sinking spells along the way, and considerable anger toward the spouse who "forced" this change upon us. The adjustment is often so difficult that we are left with insecurities that interfere with new relationships. Our fear of being alone may lead us to choose our next mate hastily and unwisely. Our fear of reassuming sole responsibility for our lives may prevent us from analyzing our own behavior and learning to act in ways that are more likely to be rewarding. And our fear of being hurt again can keep us from enjoying the intimacy necessary to be fully committed to another person.

These difficulties are complicated by the ambivalence most of us feel after divorce. Unless it was totally irrational to marry in the first place, we all have mixed feelings when the marriage ends. No matter how bad a marriage seems in retrospect, it was not all bad. So during the times when post-divorce life is particularly difficult or lonely, we often recall the good things we left behind.

Some ambivalence after divorce is inevitable. But when we can't understand and control it, confusion can complicate our lives. Unresolved attachment to our ex-spouse can interfere with the search for a new mate. Finding a new partner is difficult enough without having to overcome a strong attachment to our ex-spouse. And once we find a prospective mate, our ambivalence can be very threatening to the new relationship.

When difficulties arise, as they always will, it's easy to think back on our previous mate and idealize his or her better qualities. We risk making comparisons that are as distorted as they are useless. If we reveal the comparisons we are making, we can't help but hurt or anger our new partner. If our thoughts are kept private, we risk causing confusion and frustration when we act strangely because of comparisons we don't reveal.

Fear and ambivalence, then, are the potentially destructive emotional by-products of every divorce. To overcome fear, we need to establish a positive identity separate from our former marriage. Ambivalence can only be resolved when both positive and negative feelings of attachment are placed in proper perspective. We can't possibly bring the necessary self-assurance and optimism to a second marriage until we resolve the fear and ambivalence caused by the ending of the first.

Building Identity

When we separate from a spouse, we lose a part of our identity. Therefore, adjustment to divorce always demands the development of a new self-image. In his book *Divorce and After,* Paul Bohannan referred to the identity development challenges posed by the end of marriage as the "six stations of divorce."

Some of the changes are tangible. We must reestablish our legal independence, including our right to remarry. We must make financial changes such as dividing property and assuming sole responsibility for managing our own assets and debts. And we have to undergo a social face-lift in which we present ourselves as free agents rather than as part of a pair. These provide the outward structure of our new identity.

The other changes are psychological. We must start to accept full responsibility for our feelings, rather than holding our ex-spouses even partly accountable. No matter how abrupt, insensitive, or one-sided the termination may have seemed, we can't achieve psychological independence until our emotions are under our own control. Next, we must build a truly independent self-image that consolidates the legal, economic, social, and emotional elements of separation. Finally, if we have children, we must grapple with the challenge of parental redefinition as we adjust to custodial, financial, and emotional changes.

People develop their own plans for taking these steps toward reorientation. Some tackle legal and economic issues first, while others concentrate on social or psychological challenges. The speed and quality of the adjustment are affected by the level of economic freedom and security, and the social support from friends and family. The level of attachment to the ex-spouse also has its influence. The most important influence on adjustment, however, is the attitude with which the challenges are approached. *A positive and optimistic attitude is more powerful than any external force.*

Divorce doesn't simply have to be endured; it can be a catalyst for learning and change that can have a tremendously positive effect on our self-image. The ultimate goal of post-divorce adjustment is increased understanding, self-acceptance, and self-confidence. Once this is achieved, we can enter a new relationship with a better chance of making it work.

Resolving Ambivalence

When couples divorce, they seldom make a total exit from one another's lives. In the book *Marital Separation,* Robert Weiss describes the lingering attachment that often remains:

> Separation is an incident in the relationship of spouses rather than an ending of that relationship. It is a critically important incident, to be sure: an incident that ushers in fundamental changes in the relationship. But it is not an ending. Months after the individual has moved into a hotel room, furnished flat, a friend's apartment, or back to the parental home, the spouse is likely to remain the most important figure in his or her world. Even if the spouse has disappeared, as occasionally happens, he or she will remain vivid in the individual's

internal world, there to be harangued, entreated, and
called on to witness the devastation produced by his or
her departure.

People may be divorced, but they are seldom completely
separated. Unless both former partners feel battered and
abused by the termination of the marriage, at least one and
sometimes both harbor fantasies that they will remain
friends. And if there are children, parents are usually forced
to stay in contact, even if they would prefer to have nothing
to do with each other. In many cases, divorce is not the end
of the line, but a link in an enduring relationship chain.

Just as people may have had unequal levels of desire for
divorce, so they may have differing desires for post-divorce
contact. When one person's wish for contact far exceeds that
of the other, frustration and renewed anger may occur. Even
when contact is minimal, excessive thoughts and unresolved
feelings about the ex-spouse can be destructive. Several family researchers have attempted to measure post-separation
attachment by asking questions such as these:

1.   Do you often wonder what your ex-partner is doing?
2.   Do you still feel intense anger toward your ex?
3.   Do you often think that you and your ex should have
put in more effort or tried different ways to stay together?
4.   Do you feel extremely guilty about the impact that
divorce had on your ex?
5.   Do you have occasional sexual fantasies about your ex
or intense jealousy about his or her sexual encounters with
others?
6.   Do you feel hesitant to make a commitment to others
in the hope that reconciliation might be possible?
7.   How often do you do things intended to create a
desired effect on your ex? (such as trying to induce jealousy
or guilt)
8.   Do you try to increase contact with your ex by creating child-care or monetary crises?

9. Do you allow major life decisions to be affected by their possible impact upon your ex? (For example, deciding not to move to another city in order to stay geographically close.)

Answers to these questions give some idea of the strength of positive and negative feelings toward an ex-spouse. Positive replies to even a few of these questions signal the need for an evaluation of your attachment. Almost everyone has some lingering attachment to a former spouse, and if strong positive feelings are relatively rare and easily controlled, problems will be minimal. But if strong positive feelings about your ex-spouse interfere with your present relationship, it's important to come to terms with the past in order to put it to rest.

Understanding the Past

Even after we've overcome strong emotional attachments, we can still have a hard time gaining an accurate understanding of why the marriage failed. The main problem is that much of what we believe to be true about our experience is illusion. Samuel Johnson believed that at its best, history is romance, because we all recall events as we want to believe they happened. When the history involves disappointment in marriage, with the accompanying threats to identity and security, the distortions are greater still.

There are two sides to every breakup. We can think of "his divorce" and "her divorce" much as Jessie Bernard has written of "his" and "her" marriages. Recall the example of Alan and Martha who were both having affairs during their marriage. Alan tells everyone that Martha was unfaithful and that he began to have affairs as a defense measure. Martha, however, believes that her indiscretions did not begin until Alan's mysterious absences had been going on for some time. Each, then, has a very different view of the cause of their major marital problem.

When one marriage has ended and another begins, there are many different explanations for the end of the first marriage. Most of us select the version that we believe, and relate different accounts of that version to others depending on the effect we wish to achieve. While we don't exactly lie, we are guided more by the effect our accounts will have on the listener than by their accuracy. These various constructions of our experience can be termed "facilitative fictions." Although they are both self-preserving and self-deceiving, they are usually unintentionally so.

Let's suppose that Alan has left Martha to marry Sue, and consider the widely divergent accounts of the breakdown of the Alan-Martha marriage. There is:

1. The *Truth,* which cannot be determined;
2. what Alan believes;
3. what Alan tells Martha he believes;
4. what Alan tells Sue he believes;
5. what Alan tells others he believes;
6. what Sue believes;
7. what Sue tells Alan she believes;
8. what Sue may tell Martha she believes;
9. what Sue tells others she believes;
10. what Martha believes;
11. what Martha tells Alan she believes;
12. what Martha may tell Sue she believes; and,
13. what Martha tells others she believes.

Things are rarely even as simple as this. Beliefs change over time, and explanations vary from one telling to the next. In addition, there may be many other versions of the story as it is related to different people. For example, family and friends who had some first-hand exposure to the couple may hear a tale different than the one told to a lawyer who is litigating over custodial matters. Children may be "protected" from negative accounts or exposed to horror stories that go far beyond what the storyteller believes. Moreover, when Martha finds a new mate, a whole new set of accounts will be created to celebrate his entry into the drama.

We can often predict the biased way in which we describe our relationships. Depending on the circumstances, we tend to view our behavior as being under our own control or under the control of others. Because most of us try to maintain positive self-esteem, we are likely to accept responsibility for our behavior when it is positive and to assign responsibility to others when our actions are negative. For example, Alan does not think of himself as deceptive: he thinks he was unfaithful because Martha made him defensive with her own infidelities. On the other hand, he feels virtuous about keeping his promise of sexual exclusivity during the first years of their marriage. Thus he believes that Martha brought out his bad side while he takes credit for the good.

Like Alan, partners in distressed marriages are likely to highlight their own virtues and their partners' vices. This tendency to take credit for the good and to write off responsibility for the bad can be illustrated as follows:

HOW WE EXPLAIN BEHAVIOR

	Good Behavior	*Bad Behavior*
Our own	Our personality traits	Our partners' actions
Our partners	Our actions	Our partners' personality traits

It's important to remember that we often distort even our private understanding of events in predictably self-serving ways. As we try to analyze the marriage that failed, we must be aware of the tendency to credit the good things to our behavior and the bad things to our ex-spouses' personalities.

Nor should we commit the error of assuming the opposite: that all problems were due to our own personality deficits. This just leads to feelings of worthlessness and hopelessness. The most productive view of any situation focuses on the behaviors of each partner.

What then are the elements of an acceptable understanding of marital breakdown? A coherent view has four essential characteristics:

1.   It must recognize that both partners acted in ways that were both helpful and harmful, with neither being absolutely good or entirely bad. *Every coherent account must start by acknowledging that both partners contributed to both the good and the bad in the marriage.*

2.   It must acknowledge that each person's behavior was determined much more by the relationship than by external forces such as friends, in-laws, or job pressures. *Every coherent account must stress the role that each partner played in creating both the positive and the negative behaviors of the other.*

3.   It must accept that while outside factors may influence the relationship, partners can work together to meet the challenges they face. *Every coherent account must identify ways in which the couple cooperated and ways in which they could have worked together better to meet challenges posed by external forces.*

4.   It must be free of an effort to describe partner's behaviors in terms of general personality traits (such as "He was lazy" or "She was selfish"). Instead, *every coherent account must stress the actions that each person took under various circumstances rather than focusing on traits that each person brought to the union.*

As an aid in coming to terms with your first marriage, it can be helpful to write a short history of the relationship. If you have some unresolved feelings, try to put some of your thoughts in writing. You may want to answer the following questions:

What attracted you to each other when you met?

What led you both to decide to marry?

What did you each do to make the marriage work?

How did you each contribute to its failures?

What still makes you feel angry? How might you have contributed to the situation?

What still makes you feel guilty? How might your partner have contributed to the situation?

What did the experience teach you about yourself that will put you in a better position to have greater success in your next marriage?

When your account is written, examine it in light of the requirements for a coherent understanding. If you find that it is too biased or if it doesn't guide you toward a different approach in a second marriage, it's worth rewriting, or at least rethinking, until it serves your purpose well.

The things we do with our spouses are seldom intrinsically right or wrong: their meaning can only be understood in the context of the relationship. In addition, marital behavior is always two-sided: husbands and wives work together to achieve the things that work well and must also share responsibility for what goes wrong. We can't do anything about the mistakes our ex-partners made, but we can learn from our own mistakes. Once we acknowledge that changes in our behavior just might have altered the outcome of our first marriage, we are more likely to make our second marriage more successful. In short, we need a balanced and coherent view of history, so that we can replace past mistakes with actions which will create a future that meets our desires.

3

A Better Choice
the Second Time

WDF, 37, 2 wonderful sons. Lawyer with a
sense of humor. Loves walks in the woods,
music, dining out, and travel anywhere.
Seeks marriage-minded prof. man of like
interests.

We once believed that personal ads were placed or answered only by people with exotic sexual preferences. But now almost every newspaper offers a gallery of "sincere," "attractive," professionals who, by their own estimates, are never boring because they are thrilled by everything. And the ads are more likely to offer a lasting commitment than a kinky weekend.

Millions of Americans are more or less actively on the lookout for good prospects for a second marriage. They are supplementing the traditional blind dates and parties with personal ads, singles cruises, and health club memberships. Some methods of mate selection have a long history: astrology has always had its allure, and, as John Goodwin observed in *The Mating Trade,* more modern Americans turn to the stars for love signs in one day than was true throughout the history of ancient Greece and Rome. Other methods, such as computer and video dating services, reflect today's technology. Whatever methods are used, divorced people throughout the country are doing everything they can to find suitable second partners.

Many barriers can prevent the likelihood of meeting anyone at all, much less a good match. Some people have to spend so much time at work that they don't have time to socialize; some put so much energy into being a single parent that they are too tired to "play the field"; and others are so isolated by the anonymity of urban life that it seems impossible to meet desirable partners through casual encounters.

The quest can be difficult, though the requirements for success are straightforward: you have to find a person who seems right for you, and you have to build confidence that you've made the right decision. This seldom happens effortlessly. Most veterans of unhappy first marriages agree with Jane Carpineto who was quoted in the *New York Times* as saying: ". . . if you believe love happens when you look into someone's eyes, you'll find out later why divorce happens."

Finding a good mate takes a combination of skill, energy, and good fortune. Skill helps us increase our chances of finding the kind of person we want to meet. We can't count on stumbling onto good opportunities—we need to create them. Many people who bemoan their rotten luck don't realize they actually help to create their fate. For example, one woman complains that she only meets alcoholics, another that she only meets "exercise nuts," and a third that she only meets indigent intellectuals. When these women are asked where they go to find men, the first woman says she goes to bars, the second to a health club, and the third to poetry readings. Of course none of the women should be surprised at the men she meets, for who else is she likely to find in the places she chooses to look?

The people you meet are the ones you arrange to find, whether or not you are aware of the plan. Therefore, a good first step is to define precisely the kind of people who interest you, determine where they are likely to spend time, and arrange to be on hand to meet them.

After you have your capsule profile of the person you

want, you can proceed with varying degrees of effort. As one option, you can hope to run into that interesting someone on the block where you live or in the next office. Years ago, when it was observed that most people marry someone from the neighborhood rather than a person from the other side of town, one writer quipped that the wings of Cupid might be best adapted for short flights.

Those who don't want to count on luck to deliver the person of their dreams will risk going a bit further to find people they like. They may arrange parties rather than wait to be invited, and they may give every reasonable prospect a try. They will risk the chance of rejection inherent in dating in order to increase their chances of finding a good match. Obviously, the more effort that is invested, the greater the opportunity to improve upon what "luck" has to offer.

That's enough about first encounters. Now let's turn to what to do after curiosity turns to interest.

The woman who placed the ad at the beginning of the chapter is one of our friends who lives in a large East Coast city. Anne is a divorced, white, female, 37-year-old attorney. She met Dave at a T.G.I.F. in a bar around the corner from the university, midway through their second year of law school. Dave was a regular at the bar, explaining that he was drowning his sorrows while rebounding from the loss of another woman.

Anne and Dave dated for a year and lived together for two before they married. Even after their relationship became solid, Dave continued to drink too much. His response to Anne's expression of concern was first that he was really pressured by studies, then exams, and finally by worry about what job to take. Dave's drinking was Anne's only concern about their relationship, and she hoped that it would end as soon as their marriage was secure and they both had good jobs.

Seven years and two children later, Dave announced that

he had taken an apartment in another part of the city. There was no other woman and they rarely had a fight, so Anne was totally surprised and overwhelmed. Eventually her shock gave way to hurt, denial, fear, anger, then resignation, and finally separation.

Now that she has risen to the challenge of going it alone, Anne worries that any new relationship will eventually bring her as much pain as the one just ended. She doubts her instincts because she really did think she was the right woman for Dave and he was the right man for her. She is also worried because she didn't see the end coming, and she questions her ability to see the obvious even now.

Anne can take comfort in the knowledge that almost all divorced people under 45 will remarry if they want to. There are, however, four essential principles she must keep in mind if she is to choose wisely the second time.

Principle 1   If there is anything we very much want in a partner, we should find someone who already has it. We can't trust the power of our love to create what is not there initially.

Anne knew that Dave had a drinking problem but it didn't seem to interfere with his work. She even liked his easy sense of humor and affectionate manner when he had a few to "loosen up". She was aware that she was more concerned about drinking than he was, but she married him anyway, confident that she could convince him that too much alcohol was as bad for his health as it was for his reputation.

Unfortunately, Dave didn't marry Anne to be "improved" by her, but to enjoy her acceptance. Relationships are strengthened when partners support each other's identities, and weakened when one sets out to change the other in any significant way. The implication of this for mate selection is obvious: when certain behavior patterns are important to us, we should find a person who already has them. If the qualities we seek are lacking, we should at least try to encourage development of the new patterns before marrying. The chance of successfully promoting change later is very slim indeed.

When she came to our house for dinner one night, Anne complained that alcohol had won the contest for Dave's affections. Dave offered quite a different explanation when we had a chance to hear his side. He said: "I never dreamed our marriage would end. I loved Anne as much as I will ever love anyone. But I felt she didn't respect me and constantly implied that I was a drunken fool. I can't recall her ever leaving me alone about my drinking, or even asking how I felt about it.

"After a few years, she would put me on the witness stand every evening and ask what I had to drink that day. And she refused to make love with me if she smelled alcohol on my breath, even if we drank together at a party. The more she probed and withdrew, the angrier I became and the more I drank. I left when I realized that I'd never have her respect, and that I'd become a lush in the bargain."

As we all do, Dave wanted acceptance, but all he got was a constant demand to meet Anne's standards of behavior. Given Anne's feelings about drinking, she should have married a man whose views were similar to hers. Instead, she chose a man who thought of drinking as part of the normal course of every day.

To increase the likelihood of having what we want in marriage, we should know what we want from the start, find a person who offers what we seek, and avoid relying on attempts to mold a mate to suit our desires.

Principle 2   We shouldn't marry anyone we don't love, but we should never make the mistake of marrying for love alone.

Though many of us might have a hard time explaining exactly what love is, most of us devote a lot of time and energy to its pursuit. When we decide to marry, we usually base the decision primarily on the strength of the love we feel.

In other places and other times, love was believed to be the possible consequence of marriage but never its reasonable cause. In fact, those who study other cultures almost never refer to love. Anthropologist R.H. Lowie went so far as to express his contempt for the popular notion of love in the following terms:

> All societies recognize that there are occasional violent, emotional attachments between persons of the opposite sex, but our present American culture is practically the only one which has attempted to capitalize on these, and make them the basis for marriage. . . . The hero of the modern American movie is always a romantic lover, just as the hero of the old Arab epic is always an epileptic. A cynic may suspect that in any ordinary population, the percentage of individuals with a capacity for romantic love of the Hollywood type was about as large as that of persons able to throw a genuine epileptic fit.

This was written over 50 years ago, and modern movies are much more realistic than movies of the 30s. But the enormous popularity of modern "romance novels" provides ample evidence that the romantic ideal is alive and well even in these purportedly cynical times.

Many of us eventually recognize the tendency to confuse infatuation with love, but we don't always use this distinction when we need it most. Infatuation exists when we become ecstatic about another person whom we hardly know; when our interest rises in response to the other's disinterest and falls when intimacy grows; and when thoughts about the other person make almost everything else in our lives pale in importance. Love is a more mellow feeling, but one that holds the promise of prolonged satisfaction because it is based upon true knowledge of our partner and a genuine sharing of interests and commitment.

These days, we are expected to find our own partners, differentiate between infatuation and love, and then base our decision to marry upon the unmeasurable strength of our

love. We do this even though many believe that love is blind
and can't be trusted, and despite the possibility that we may
be more in love with love than with our partners. In addition,
most of us will fall in love more than once: we don't necessarily marry the one we love the most, but the one who is most
loved at the time we decide to marry.

If love is a feeling of someone being as important to us as
we are to ourselves, it is essential to a good marriage. Alexander Pope has called love "the careful, honest, giving over
of ourselves to knowing another human being even as we are
known . . . no matter how flawed both may be." Still, the bills
must be paid, the chores done, and the other challenges of
daily living met. When two people have incompatible ways
of handling many of the details of their lives, their daily
routines can be a constant struggle. If their goals and values
are very different, a satisfying long-term commitment will
elude them. Love is necessary, but it's never enough to insure
a happy marriage.

*Principle 3   While we may be stimulated by people
who are different from us, those most like us tend to
be better choices as mates.*

There are two conflicting views about what we look for when
choosing a spouse. Some believe that opposites attract; they
claim that we seek out people who are different from us in
complementary ways. For example, if we are dominant, we
like people who are submissive; if we are messy, we are
attracted to people who are neat; and if we are shy, we prefer
people who are outgoing. Interesting though the notion of
complements may be, it has received virtually no support.
Instead, most researchers find that we are more comfortable
with people who are similar to us, and we are uncomfortable
with those who are different.

People who bring very different values to marriage are in
for potential conflict. Whenever differences of opinion arise,
whether significant or not, we try to change each other's

minds, and are resentful when we fail. We want our partners to agree with the beliefs we hold most strongly, and we feel personally rejected when our core ideas are not accepted. While debates may be interesting for a while, we soon tire of the pressure to constantly defend our core beliefs.

When we hold the same values as our partners, we can be more spontaneous, with confidence that we'll share the same likes and dislikes. Counting on mutual agreement, we can bypass the effort it takes to argue over basic principles before making each decision. Equally important, agreement leads us to feel appreciated and valued by each other. As we will see in later chapters, this kind of acceptance is at the root of a good and lasting relationship.

Because there is such comfort and ease in likeness, it should not be surprising that we usually marry people similar to us in age, appearance, mental health, comfort with novelty, religion, and important values. The more accurate we are about our perceived similarity to our partners, the more likely we are to create a happy and stable marriage.

A study of husband-wife differences among one group of couples who married only once, and another that had undergone *two* divorces reached some very interesting conclusions. Spouses who remained in their first marriages were more alike in age, education, and religion than those who divorced. And those who ended their second marriages consistently chose mates who had still more than the average expected differences in these and related areas. Partners who have different values and life experiences seem to face a more difficult adjustment than those who have more in common.

Still, despite the importance of similarity, most of us seek more than an opposite-sex version of ourselves. Too much similarity can be boring. We need someone who shares our important values, but who is different enough to broaden our perspective and make life interesting. The similarities make life easier, while the differences make it more productive and stimulating. We should be like our partners in broad brush strokes, but different in fine detail.

Principle 4   Marry for yourself, not for anyone else.

In olden days, when parents still had influence over their children, children sometimes married to please their parents instead of then.selves. It was unusual to marry someone "from the other side of the tracks" even if that was the person most loved. For reasons ranging from respect for parents' wishes to fear of their reprisals, children allowed their parents to play a significant role in the selection of their mates.

These days, parents may feel lucky if they have the chance to meet their child's "intended" before the commitment to marry is made. Parental wishes are seldom heeded, and in fact, many parents refrain from expressing too much dismay or enthusiasm, lest the child feel the need to rebel. But when second marriages are being contemplated, family needs may take precedence over individual desires, just as they did in times past. The difference is that people considering remarriage are concerned with pleasing their children instead of their parents. A custodial parent will surely look for someone who will be a good stepparent. And if the children are very fond of someone who falls far short of their parent's ideal, the parent may try to create love where none exists. But a parent must live with the new partner long after the children leave. Despite the temptation to put the children's needs before everything else, we all must make our own choices about whom to marry.

Because we all realize that instinct, chemistry, or family approval may not be the most reliable criteria for choosing a new mate, most people look for other ways to evaluate the wisdom of their choices. The exercises that follow will be of particular interest to those who have not yet remarried, because they contain guidelines for self-analysis and for evaluating the qualities you want in a relationship. Couples who have already remarried but who would like more insight into their choices may also find them useful.

It is best if both partners complete each exercise separately, and then discuss the results together. Although it's important to note areas of agreement or disagreement, it should be stressed that agreement does not guarantee marital bliss any more than disagreement forecasts marital strife. The information is simply a springboard for productive discussion.

Before you can evaluate your choice of a prospective mate, you need to be aware of how you are "marketing" yourself, and what you are expecting in return. One way to help you clarify what you want is to write a hypothetical personals ad. In it, you should describe the kind of person you'd like to find, and what you offer in return. List in your ad any requirements or strong preferences you have for a mate. The description may include age, occupational status, religion, personality characteristics, and anything else you consider to be important. Then write a description of yourself that honestly conveys the way you present yourself to others. Don't worry about style. In the "real" personals, it's important to catch the reader's attention. In this exercise, the focus is on content rather than style. A simple and direct expression of your own preferences and qualities is all you need.

MY PERSONAL AD

Who I want to meet.

What I offer in exchange.

Look over your ad. Underline the traits you have selected for a partner and the key elements in the statements you made about yourself. Is your self-description accurate? Would people who know you well use the same words to describe you? In painting a picture of the partner you seek, have you been too idealistic? Are the traits you seek in a partner compatible with what you have to offer? Have you advertised for the perfect date instead of the perfect mate? Should you add any qualities that you consider essential in a spouse?

Then exchange ads with your partner. Do you find each other's self-descriptions accurate? Do you both mention many of the same things? To what extent do you feel you meet each other's descriptions of the ideal mate? Has either of you mentioned qualities that the other lacks? Is there a good balance between what is offered and what is expected?

Whether or not we actually write an ad, we are all marketing ourselves as we search for a new partner. Effective marketing will necessarily focus on and perhaps even exaggerate the positive points, while minimizing or ignoring the negative ones. It's important for us to be aware of characteristics we choose to stress in selling ourselves, and to make sure our expectations are reasonably consistent with what we have to offer.

In courtship, we seldom think about choosing the goals we will use to structure our lives, but once married, our goals and priorities strongly influence the nature of the marriage. The next exercise will help you specify the goals that are most important to you, and those you would like your spouse to consider important.

Choosing Life Goals

Listed on page 48 are commonly mentioned life goals. Read through the list and add any of your own that don't appear. Then use the left-hand column to note the importance of each goal to you personally, and use the right-hand column to rank how important it is for you that your partner achieve each goal. For simplicity, *choose no more than four goals in the "Most Important" category for yourself and four for your partner.*

Consider the ranking of your own goals. Have you based your evaluations on your actions instead of your intentions? Our partners are more interested in what we do than what we say. For example, nearly everyone planning to marry states that "spending time together" is a high priority, but many of these people also take jobs that require late hours and frequent travel which leave little time for their new mates. And many people who "feel committed" to spending several hours every day with their children actually use their nonworking time to take extra courses, pursue self-development projects or see adult friends. Conflicts like these between stated goals and actual behavior create confusion and can trigger eventual conflict.

We should also keep in mind that just as we sometimes fall short of our self-selected objectives, so, too, do others. In comparing ourselves with others, it is important to avoid the trap of thinking in terms of *our intentions* and *their behavior.* We should focus on our own behavior as well as that of our partners.

Not everyone wants a spouse whose priorities are identical to their own. It's perfectly acceptable for people to have different objectives as long as they express them openly and are willing to compromise if that becomes necessary to keep the marriage happy and stable. As an example, achieving financial security may be of prime importance to either the husband or the wife, while development of a creative talent may be the most important goal of the other. The couple would be in trouble if the spouse seeking financial security expects the other to earn a lot of money, while the one seeking artistic growth wants financial support for self-development efforts that preclude working. On the other hand, they could reach an agreement in which one takes 90 percent of the responsibility for earning money—and is free

Importance for me to achieve goal			Goal	Importance for my partner to achieve goal		
Most	Somewhat	Not		Most	Somewhat	Not
			Financial security			
			Raising a family			
			A spiritual or religious commitment			
			Spending time together			
			Intellectual development			
			Professional growth			
			Travel			
			Health and physical fitness			
			Community work			
			Close contact with parents, and other family			

to use all the time it takes—while the other is free to devote as much time as needed to cultivate a talent. Having the same priorities is not essential as long as both partners agree to the same distribution of responsibilities.

Not all differences in goals can be resolved by negotiating responsibilities. For example, if one spouse puts career development above all else, while the other feels that spending a lot of time together is most important, they may eventually face intense conflict. Major differences in goals can be so fundamental that they seriously undermine the potential for a happy marriage. The best way to deal with such issues is to discuss them frankly, allowing each person to make a decision as to whether the goal or the marriage is more important. For example, one husband who wanted to start a business that would require extensive travel decided that increased income would not compensate for the frustration of his wife, who felt she could not accept frequent separations. Adjustments such as these need not be viewed as a personal sacrifice as long as important goals are shared.

The next exercise will focus on making the most of what you learned about your former marriage. Most people who remarry look for new partners who are very different from their former mates in areas that were the greatest source of concern. In *The Divorce Experience,* Morton and Bernice Hunt state that: ". . . the large majority of the formerly married people tend to withdraw from new potential partners if, as they become intimate with them, they recognize the old familiar traits that made trouble in the first marriage. Whether they choose well or poorly, the second marriage is rarely a copy of the first."

In the previous chapter, the development of a coherent view of your first marriage was discussed. Now it's time to compare what you learned about your first partner with judgments you've made about your new one.

The following form is derived from the work of psychologist George Kelly. It is part of our more comprehensive computer-scored premarital assessment inventory which can be ordered from Compuscore, Box 7035, Ann Arbor, Michigan, 48107. This version will help you organize your views about your own most and least valued characteristics, those of your past partner, and those of your present or prospective mate. As before, you and your partner should complete this form separately.

Characteristics of Self and Partners

In the first column on the next page, list *eight* qualities that you *most like* to find in the important people in your life. These could include behavior patterns (e.g., "loves children" or "doesn't smoke") or personality characteristics (e.g., "kindness" or "intelligence"). Then list *four* qualities that you do *not like* to see in people who are important to you.

Under the column headed "Yourself," write a number on a scale between 5 (almost always true) and 1 (almost never true) to indicate how well you think this characteristic applies to you. Then do the same for the columns headed "Former Partner" and "New Partner."

You and your partner should complete this exercise separately, and share only as much as you wish with each other. Score each of your assessments (self, former partner, new partner) by:

1. Adding all of the numbers assigned to positive qualities and entering sum on positive subtotal line.
2. Adding all of the numbers assigned to negative qualities and entering on negative subtotal line.
3. Subtracting the negative subtotal from the positive subtotal and entering on the "Total" line.

When you compare one person with another (e.g., your first spouse and your present partner, or yourself and your present partner), a difference of 12 or more points on the "Total" line is significant. You probably *want* to find a sig-

Characteristic	Yourself	Former Partner	New Partner
Positive Qualities	5-4-3-2-1	5-4-3-2-1	5-4-3-2-1
1			
2			
3			
4			
5			
6			
7			
8			
Subtotal			
Negative Qualities			
1			
2			
3			
4			
Positive Subtotal			
Negative Subtotal			
Total			

nificant difference between your present and past partners; that would seem only natural. But you don't want to find a significant difference between yourself and your present partner. Here you are in the best shape if both evaluations are similar and relatively high. In a good relationship, partners are in power-equal positions. If one person is rated much more positively than the other, that person generally has much more power. Such an imbalance never works to either partner's long-term advantage. If you or your partner find a significant difference between the self-rating and partner rating, you should work toward achieving more balance.

Some people are surprised to find that they still view their former partners in positive terms. Others are struck by how little they value the dear departed. Both reactions are understandable. However, as noted earlier, a balanced view of the good and bad has much more to offer than can be found at either extreme.

Don't be alarmed if you discover similarities between your present and past partner. It's natural to look for and find similar positive attributes. But when negatives are repeated, it's wise to consider better ways of handling difficulties the second time around.

While many divorced people learn the importance of choosing mates wisely, some are so anxious to be married again that they throw caution to the wind once they meet someone who is willing to make a commitment. While they may be aware of flaws in their prospective partners, they underestimate the seriousness of the liabilities and hope that the new mates will improve after marriage. Some problems, of course, are resolved once newlyweds learn to understand each other. But others grow worse after the honeymoon is over.

In general, it isn't a good idea to compromise too much in making a decision to marry. Major problems should always be resolved *before* you commit to spend your life with another person. Many people look back at their first marriages and say they knew from the beginning that there would be trouble: this is a mistake that need not be repeated.

Why do so many people seem continually to make poor choices? Many choose to stay with familiar patterns rather than facing the uncertainty of adjusting to new ones. Some women (often the daughters of abusive and/or alcoholic parents) learn to tolerate abuse or alcoholism in their husbands. In a similar pattern, many men whose first wives were unfaithful find themselves faced with infidelity in their new marriages. They go from one mate to the next, exchanging the packaging but never the poor contents.

If you find yourself repeating an inappropriate choice, it's time to give serious attention to alternatives. It's helpful to examine the role that your partner's negative behavior might play in your life. For example, one of our clients complained that both her present and former husbands were violent. While their aggression was inexcusable, it was also understandable. The woman had tremendous doubts about her worth as a person and she was most comfortable with men to whom she felt superior. She frequently avoided her current husband and otherwise treated him with disdain. As a result, he felt driven to do whatever he could (however destructive the behavior might be) to re-establish his own self-esteem.

The husband in another couple we treated complained that both his first and second wives gained a considerable amount of weight once he became involved with them. He viewed this as a hostile act, and he bemoaned his bad luck with women. Further discussion revealed that this man was sexually impotent in both relationships and he blamed his erectile problem on his partners' lack of physical appeal.

If negative patterns are suspected, the help of a therapist is recommended. We were able to help each of these people recognize their own role in creating their marital problems, and we helped the spouses work together to create more rewarding marriages. While counseling before remarriage is preferable, therapy can also promote valuable change after problems arise in the new marriage.

Even if you marry a person who has every quality you desire, you'll still run into trouble if your kind and thoughtful spouse thinks a woman's place is in the home and you believe women should share the benefits and responsibilities of earning a living. Beliefs about sex roles are another important factor to consider when choosing a mate. Running conflicts over who should take on which responsibilities can put a real strain on a marriage. In several studies, spouses were asked whether they would marry the same person again. The willingness to do so was very strongly influenced by the level of agreement about the roles of husband and wife. Finding and marrying someone with views consistent with yours is much easier than trying to negotiate agreement after marriage.

Divorce often changes expectations about the roles of husband and wife. While both men and women who remarry appear to favor greater equality in the new marriage, women marrying for the second time feel more strongly about this. Their views about the roles of wife and mother are generally less traditional than when they first said "I do." Because our beliefs about sex roles are often very firmly established, it's important that partners compare their views and attempt to find a reasonable compromise if differences exist. This issue will be discussed in much greater detail in Chapter 8, when we come to the division of home and work responsibilities.

While many decisions are amenable to negotiation, the decision about whether to have children is not. Nowadays, when more and more people are living together without marriage, the desire to have children can be one of the principal motivations to marry. Yet an increasing number of people feel that children are not necessary for a satisfying marriage, and many remarrying men and women already have children and want no more. Now that it's no longer a foregone conclusion that marriage means children, it's particularly important for remarrying couples to decide before they marry whether or not to have children. Of course, either or both partners might have a change of heart later, but it's a design for disaster if people begin a marriage with strong differences on this issue. The following questions will help you assess and compare your attitudes about children.

Attitudes Toward Children

How strongly do you agree or disagree with each of the following statements?

How do you think your partner will respond to the following statements?

> 5 Strongly agree
> 4 Agree
> 3 Neutral
> 2 Disagree
> 1 Strongly disagree

1.   I would not marry unless I could expect to become a parent with my new partner.
2.   I consider it my duty to have as many children as I can.
3.   I do not believe that husbands and wives who choose to be childless can be as happy as those who have children.
4.   I am willing to assume almost all of the responsibility for the care of our children.
5.   I have always looked forward to becoming a parent.
6.   I greatly enjoy doing things with and for children of all ages.
7.   I expect to be happy in meeting my child's needs before meeting my own.

How many questions do you and your partner answer the same way? This is a measure of your agreement. How accurately do you and your partner predict one another's answers? This is a measure of your understanding of one another's position.

Among the various assessment exercises offered here, none

is more important than this one concerning children. The desire to procreate is powerful in many men and women, but very low in others—especially those who already have children. People who do want children are likely to feel cheated if the parenthood years pass without any births. Those who don't want children and then become parents are likely to feel oppressed and overburdened. For these reasons, and because the biological clock for women sets an absolute time limit for discussion of this issue, it is one spouse-selection issue that demands absolutely honest self-disclosure and the highest possible level of understanding and agreement.

All of the issues addressed in these exercises are important, and for some couples, they may be the quintessential points. For others, however, concerns such as fidelity, independence, or relationships with friends and family may be the most important ones. Frank discussion of these concerns will increase the chances of marital happiness.

By identifying and reaching agreement on basic values, you and your partner can take an important first step in preparing for a good second marriage. But since values are so vague, there is a vast amount of room for individual interpretation. Couples who are anticipating marriage will naturally try to present themselves as positively as possible, without being aware of the consequences. They are also likely to idealize each other, glossing over any suspicion of potential problems in the hope that time and love will work them out. These presentations and interpretations can set the new relationship on a very weak foundation. In the next chapter we'll discuss the deliberate and unintentional deceptions that enhance courtship but endanger marriage.

4

Uncovering Secret Contracts

Courtship is the time of maximum human deception. Never during the course of human development do we overstate our virtues or conceal our vices as skillfully as we do when we try to convince someone to share our lives.

We are not alone. Many animals put on exaggerated displays in order to gain an opportunity to reproduce. Like these animals, humans engage in courtship rituals to attract attention and win favor. But we differ from other animals in two important ways. Rejected animals seem to turn immediately to courting another prospective partner, while we are more likely to go into mourning. And while animals rarely have contact with one another after fertilization, courtship is just an early stage of a long-term relationship for humans. Only people allow courtship to affect their self-esteem and their expectations for the future.

Our forefathers were very suspicious of courtship. In 1647, the Massachusetts legislature believed that courtship should be regulated by law, claiming that it was a process in which "young men . . . watch all advantages for their evil purposes, to insinuate [themselves] into the affections of young maidens. . . ." Others did not see courtship as an evil, but they believed it had little to do with the realities of marriage. William Congreve warned that "courtship is to marriage as a very witty prologue is to a very dull play" and Alexander Pope observed "they dream in courtship, but in wedlock wake."

"To court" means "to allure, to tempt . . . to seek to attract by attentions and flatteries . . . leading to engagement and marriage." The definition of the word makes it clear that courtship is not intended to provide a couple with a realistic picture of a lifetime together, but simply to increase the likelihood that the couple will marry. It's only natural, then, that men and women who are courting present themselves in the most positive light.

Courtship patterns have changed through the ages, and many people nowadays try very hard to "be themselves" as they get to know a prospective mate. If we've been married before, we're particularly skeptical about those appealing images we see in courtship. One major disappointment is enough to convince us that courtship promises may have little to do with marriage realities. But most of us eventually find dating more disappointing than fulfilling, and we long for the comfort and security of a more permanent and stable relationship. So we are willing to set our doubts aside, idealizing what we can, rationalizing flaws we can't deny, and doing our best to convince ourselves that *this* person is the *right* person.

As soon as we decide that we want this relationship to work, we start trying harder to please. We do our best to create a good impression, trying to earn as much affection, respect, and trust as we can. We display table manners that may never be seen again. We bone up on books and current events that will never earn our notice in the future. We take pains to laugh at our dates' jokes, no matter how corny they may seem. And we feign interest in anything from basketball games to ballet just to show that we like the same things. We don't want to lie, but neither do we want to emphasize our liabilities. Since we are trying to sell ourselves, we carefully choose what to reveal about our past. When we talk about our first marriages, we describe our heroic efforts to make things work and our spouses' failure to do anything to help. And we talk more about how well our children did in school than how much trouble they have caused at home. Everything we do is intended to create an aura conducive to "I will" rather than "How could you even ask?"

Since many people no longer trust the dating process, they choose to live together in an attempt to get a more accurate idea of what the future would hold. Unfortunately, couples who live together before marriage are no less likely to divorce than those who don't. This suggests that even 24-hour contact for months or even years is insufficient to convey the truth about life after marriage.

People live together in good faith, without deliberately planning to deceive. But cohabitation is different from marriage in important ways. Palimony suits notwithstanding, cohabiting couples have fewer legal and social ties than those that bind married couples. Families, friends, and religious leaders who often pressure a married couple to stay together may actually feel relieved when a cohabiting pair splits up. And the partners agree to stay together only as long as both are happy. Because they know that the relationship can be ended as soon as either loses interest, both are motivated to make a constant effort to keep the satisfaction level high.

Marriage offers a very different commitment. We speak vows that are unconditional, promising to maintain the bond "as long as we both shall live" not "as long as we both are happy." This unconditional promise often allows married couples to feel less obligation to continue to work on the relationship. Once the goal is reached and the marriage vows exchanged, attention can be turned to other concerns. All too often, we unwittingly rely upon social, religious, and legal forces to preserve the marriage. Unfortunately, while outside forces may be strong enough to keep the marriage intact, only the partners' efforts can make it happy.

Assumptions made on the basis of courtship behaviors, with or without cohabitation, often create problems that can eventually sabotage marriage. We naively interpret courtship behaviors as promises that our partners will be as eager to please us after marriage as before. We engage in a bit of benevolent self-deception in which we assume that our partners plan to continue to deliver, but we never check out our assumptions. We want so much to believe all is well that we decide to act as if it is.

As a result, we think we have our partners' promise to continue courtship behavior even though we realize that we have made no such commitment ourselves. The commitment is assumed and never verified, but we act as though it were as binding as a formal vow. Unfortunately, because these expectations are never discussed, they may be false. For example, during courtship he may regularly prepare gourmet meals for her, leading her to expect more of the same when they marry. Imagine her surprise and disappointment when he comes home with carry-out fast foods on his nights to cook.

Since most of us consider courtship to be a preview of the coming marriage, why aren't we more open about our expectations? Often, we are too embarrassed to discuss our wishes in detail. For example, we may be reluctant to prescribe the way we want our partners to express affection, approach us sexually, or manage their personal hygiene. We would rather just assume that our desires will be met. Unfortunately, the fact that we never asked for the things we didn't get does not minimize our disappointment when they aren't delivered.

Many of us are also reluctant to create a debt that has to be repaid. As long as we don't ask for what we want, we can feel less responsible for reciprocating when we get it. Although we operate on a pay-for-what-you receive basis in business, we expect good behavior from our spouses as a matter of right, whether or not we meet their desires in return. This belief inevitably causes problems.

Finally, we often fail to discuss important issues before we marry simply because it never occurs to us to do so. We are so taken up with the romantic excitement of courtship that we don't consider details like who will be bringing home the bacon, or who will clean the refrigerator in which it is kept.

We pay a heavy price for not discussing what we have and what we want. Whether we realize it or not, *everything that we do in courtship is understood to be an implicit promise to continue to act the same way throughout the marriage.* Our expectations of marriage are based much more upon behavior than intent.

How binding can these premarital secret agreements be? Life does not stand still, and we can't be expected to act on our silver anniversaries the same way we did on our wedding nights. Change in behavior over the years is not only unavoidable, it is even desirable. But when a behavioral change implies a change in basic values, the marriage can be threatened.

While it's expected that we will handle the details of our lives differently over time, we have a responsibility to base any changes in behavior on a consistent set of principles. We *should discuss* any plans to change our behavior, but we *must negotiate* any shift in values.

Values are the superstructure of our lives, the general principles that guide our answers to the important questions we face throughout the years. Value decisions relevant to marriage might include: the relative importance of home and work, the importance of a sexually exclusive relationship, the amount of openness and sharing desired, concern for a healthy way of living, the role of religion in the couple's life, and expectations concerning independence versus interdependence. It's reasonable for courting couples to hold one another accountable for the values expressed before marriage, although the ways in which these values are acted upon may vary according to the constraints and opportunities that emerge over time.

Let's see how this looks in the example of one couple. Ken's first marriage had been a traditional one. His wife stayed home and raised the children while he worked hard to provide the financial support. As the years went by, Ken felt more and more oppressed. It seemed that no matter how much money he made, his family always wanted more. He also felt that any time he wasn't at work, he was expected to do something for one child or the other. In his opinion, he was not appreciated as a person, but only as a breadwinner, tutor, and chauffeur.

Then Ken met June at a friend's party, and he was immediately entranced. June was young, dynamic, divorced, and powerfully attracted to him. She had been married for three years and had a child who was living with his father. As the story so often goes, Ken eventually divorced his first wife and married June. He was exhilarated at having the opportunity to recapture some of his lost youth, and he luxuriated in the freedom of not being a full-time parent.

His ecstasy with June continued for about a year. Then, on her 32nd birthday, June told Ken that she wanted her son to live with them, and she also wanted to move from the city to the suburbs. She intended to continue to work part time, but she planned to combine work with motherhood.

Ken felt his new lease on life had been cruelly shattered. He had already put in his time as a father, and he didn't want another cycle of hours behind the wheel and endless struggles to find excuses for not being a Little League coach, assistant scout master, debate judge, or host for the graduation beer-bust. Even more important, he feared that June, like his first wife, would neglect him in favor of her son.

For her part, June had always believed that Ken was a man who basically enjoyed fatherhood but who just needed to experience it with a more appreciative spouse. Her work was important, but she expected to feel complete only after she became a full-time mother again. The ensuing struggle between Ken and June left them both with very bad feelings as each held the other accountable for deliberate deception.

How is it that Ken and June managed to avoid discussing this crucial issue before they decided to marry? Certainly each must have had some idea that the issue of child custody could arise again. But in order to keep each other happy, as courting couples must do, they avoided detailed discussions about issues where they feared disagreement. They spoke less often and less emphatically about their own expectations, and they interpreted each other's messages in the most positive way. For example, when Ken heard June describe her pleasure at being alone with him, he felt sure she was saying that she was happy to devote all of her attention to him. When June saw the pride Ken took in her son's accomplishments, she was sure he wouldn't mind having him live with them. The process of drawing self-serving conclusions from our partners' words and actions almost guarantees a trouble-making secret contract.

Ken and June could have guarded against this misunderstanding by an early discussion of their long-term expectations about work, children, and where to live. Talking about these issues was not without its risks: they might have decided not to marry, because being free of children now was as important to Ken as reuniting with her son was to June. But if neither was willing to negotiate on this issue, they should have tried to make that clear before they married.

Another couple had a different problem involving mismatched expectations. Ted and Ellen met when they were both management trainees, soon fell in love, and started to live together. They lived together very well, with equal sharing of nearly every aspect of their lives. Ellen cooked during the week and Ted cleaned up. Ted cooked weekend meals or arranged for dinner out. He took care of the laundry and garbage; she serviced their cars. She found and paid someone to clean their apartment; he paid the bills and prepared their taxes.

When Ted was offered a good job in another state, they decided to marry and make the move together, even though Ellen knew she might not be able to find a job. Soon after they married, they started arguing over who should do the grocery shopping, who should mow the lawn, who should prepare the meals and clean up afterward. Ellen maintained that they should share the chores as they had done before, but after marriage Ted seemed to think that fresh vegetables grew in the refrigerator and dishtowels were designed to fit only a woman's hands. Ted said he had been brought up to believe that the wife should take care of the home when the husband is the primary wage-earner. Ellen felt she had already sacrificed a good job to the relationship, and she had no intention of adding the responsibilities of a full-time housewife to her burden.

Neither Ted nor Ellen was acting in bad faith, although each accused the other of having made false promises about marriage while they were living together. They were eventually able to negotiate an agreement about household responsibilities, but if they had done it before they married, they could have prevented months of bickering.

Bargaining done before marriage helps both partners make informed decisions about whether to marry. When it occurs after marriage, the process is made more complicated by the anger that often develops when expectations haven't been met. Still, the uncovering of secret contracts can be useful at any stage of a relationship.

The secret contract is as powerful as it is unknown. We can start by defining it as precisely as we can:

A secret contract is the belief by courting partners that each will continue to act after marriage in accordance with the values and patterns established at the time they agreed to wed. It is understood that the values will prevail throughout their life together, while the daily patterns will continue until circumstances or open discussion necessitate change.

Why is it that so many of us break these implicit promises and change for the worse after we marry? After all, people can't be so devious as to deliberately put on an act only until they have "caught" a mate. And yet, it does seem that we often stop trying to please once the knot is tied.

One reason may be that courtship, though wonderful, takes tremendous effort. If courtship is to be successful, the relationship usually has to come first. Work, family, friends, and personal development may be neglected while we focus on our prospective spouses. Once married, we often tend to drift back to business as usual; consequently, the new spouses get less attention than courtship would have led them to expect.

Also, after we have formally made a lifetime commitment to another person, a question that we seldom ask while courting comes to mind, namely: "Do I want to live with this behavior for the rest of my life?" Many actions that seemed trivial or only mildly annoying during courtship become oppressive when we think in terms of living with them for a lifetime. And yet, it's easy to understand the anger that can result from having your spouse suddenly tell you that many of the things you thought were acceptable are annoying and ought to be changed.

We also change because circumstances change. People move, change jobs, make new friends, have children, get sick, and undergo the normal transitions of aging. It's foolish to expect that patterns established at age 25 will be equally feasible or even as desirable at age 55.

Let's look at a brief example of how secret contracts can change in response to new opportunities. During the time they lived together, Dan was a student and had many hours to spend with Liz. She worked full-time, but didn't really enjoy her job and rarely took work home from the office, so her evenings were also free. After they were married, Dan landed a well-paying job which kept him busy from early morning until at least nine most nights. When Dan's income increased, Liz decided to cut back and work part-time. But Dan's free time was at a premium, just when Liz expected to see more of him. He felt that she had become demanding and insensitive, while Liz felt that Dan had become self-absorbed and indifferent. Each accused the other of breaking courtship promises, when they were really both adapting to a change in circumstances. What they needed to do was find new ways to give each other caring and attention that didn't depend on large amounts of shared time.

As if the normal complications aren't bad enough, remarrying couples have a special problem. We sometimes expect our second spouses to act the same way our first partners did. We're as likely to expect the good things as the bad, and both expectations can lead to trouble. For example, Brenda's first husband reacted with fury when she talked to other men at parties they attended together, but he never cared who she saw when they were apart. Without ever asking, Brenda assumed that her second husband had similar views. During their courtship, she always stayed by his side at parties, but she made lunch "dates" with friends of both sexes. After they were married, her husband began to complain about her lunches with male friends. Brenda was initially dismayed, and she accused him of being jealous and possessive. But further discussion revealed that there were many areas in which he was not the least bit jealous. For example, he didn't care at all who she talked to at parties, and in fact preferred that they mingle separately. Her misunderstanding was not over the rules of the game, but about which players were in the game.

Whatever the cause, partners feel angry when secret agreements are broken. The anger is inappropriate, because there never was an explicit agreement, so there could not be a deliberate violation. But frustration over the inability to talk about a concern will eventually lead to anger. And the arguments that result are hard to resolve because the partners invariably have two very different ideas of the terms of the initial agreements.

When the content of these implicit agreements is revealed, each person can offer to act in certain ways and can request the kinds of responses he or she desires in exchange. When the agreement is explicit, further discussion and amendment are possible.

The form below can help you and your partner record the details of the promises you think you heard or know you want from each other. A written document has the advantage of making it easier for both partners to be sure of what is and is not expected. It's also easier for some people to put expectations in writing rather than talk about them.

Nothing should be censored from this list: include everything that is important to you. Very often, the things you are most self-conscious about discussing are the ones you are the least willing to do without. Answer these questions separately and then discuss each expectation with your partner, agreeing to those that are acceptable and negotiating compromises for those that are not.

Bear in mind that this exercise is not risk free: you may discover differences that seem alarming. Those who are considering remarriage can use the exercise to discover and openly resolve differences before marriage. Those who are already remarried can use this exercise to uncover unstated expectations that may be at the core of recurring conflicts.

Secret Contract Expectations

In what ways do you think you and your partner have agreed to handle the following issues?

1. Ownership of property and other assets.

2. Management of household responsibilities.

3. Deciding how to spend money.

4. Use of free time.

5. The role of religion in your lives.

6. The role of relatives in your lives, including parents, siblings, former spouses, and children by former marriages.

7. Your plans to have, or not to have, children.

8. Management of the use of alcohol and other drugs.

9. Management of personal health and appearance.

10. Development of independent and mutual personal interests.

11. The role and importance of friends in your lives.

12. Ways of expressing affection.

13. Details of sexual expression.

14. Extramarital sex.

15. Education and professional development.

16. Any other important issues: (specify)

When you have both identified your expectations, compare your lists. You should give each other precise descriptions of each item you list. For example, "Talk to my mother when she calls on Sundays" is much less ambiguous than "Be nice to my family." Then each of you should describe the extent to which you are willing to meet the other's expectations.

During this discussion, you will find many areas in which you accurately understand each other's desires, and are happy to meet them. You may also find some areas of disagreement. It's worth taking the time and risk needed to negotiate your differences, because after secret contracts have been revealed, they can be replaced by realistic expectations.

Let's look at an example of how one couple we saw benefitted from this exercise. Karen and Todd met each other when they were both unhappily married to other people. Eventually, they ended their marriages and began to discuss a formal commitment to each other. When they saw us for premarital counseling, they were both clearly under the spell of new love, but they also wanted to make sure that their second marriage would be more rewarding than the first.

As they completed the secret contract exercise, they were surprised to discover a number of issues they hadn't thought about. They knew they agreed about the importance of religion, family, and attention to personal fitness, but they had never discussed the way they would manage money or free time after marriage. Todd was still recoiling from his divorce settlement, and he favored the idea of keeping his remaining assets in his name only. Since Karen was successfully self-employed (and had given her ex-husband a large share of her assets in order to be free of the relationship), he assumed that she, too, would prefer separate ownership. Karen, as it turned out, believed in sharing everything, and she had interpreted Todd's generosity during courtship as a statement that he felt the same way.

This couple's expectations about free time also differed.

When Karen and Todd were in their first marriages, it was difficult for them to see each other, and they took advantage of every opportunity. Todd expected Karen to continue to spend as much time with him as possible, while Karen believed that too much time together would create the same unhealthy dependency she had in her first marriage.

Because Todd and Karen were eager to please each other and to make the relationship work, and because they had never argued about time or money, they were able to discuss their differences and work out compromises that suited them both. They decided to share most, but not all, of their assets, and they agreed to an amount of time together that each felt was acceptable though not ideal. Each felt more confident about entering a second marriage once they had worked out some of the potentially difficult details.

If you have trouble negotiating differences, we suggest that you finish the book and then come back to the problem issues. The remaining chapters are devoted to helping you understand and resolve the difficulties that often crop up in second marriages. The process of identifying and meeting these challenges is an excellent way of strengthening your marriage. Developing the ability to understand each other's views and reach mutually satisfying compromises is the best guarantee that you'll like what you get in your second marriage.

5
Managing Money in Second Marriages

At the start of a first marriage, managing money is rarely a problem. Both spouses are usually young and just beginning careers. They often bring few assets to the marriage and work for entry-level wages with little left for saving. And while there may be school debts or car payments, they have no long-term financial obligations to other people.

In contrast, money management in second marriages can be something of a nightmare. The spouses are older and at least one probably has an established career. Both usually have assets that were not jointly earned. And at least one partner often brings a complex set of financial entanglements with a former spouse.

When there are children from a first marriage, their financial support is a further complication. Since no more than one in ten children lives with a biological father and a stepmother, the typical remarrying father will come to his new bride with anywhere from two to twenty years of obligation to give money to another woman every month—or for life if alimony is involved. And if the new wife is a custodial mother, her new husband must live with the discomfort of knowing that his household is at least partially supported by another man. He will probably also be expected to contribute to the support of children who are not his own.

All of these financial ties to the first marriage can become major sources of stress in the second. Those who pay child support or alimony always feel they pay too much. Those who receive these funds always feel they are inadequate. Former spouses who manage every other issue in a friendly way may fight like wild animals over who should pay a $25 bill that easily could be either person's obligation. This dissipates energy from the new marriage, replacing it with frustration, resentment, and at least a bit of fear that the demon might strike again.

If we treated money merely as a means of making ends meet and buying a few luxuries, the problem would not be crucial. But money has symbolic meaning far beyond its economic reality. Aristotle considered a man to be happy if he had "perfect virtue" and was "adequately furnished with external goods." In his book *The Sense of Well Being in America,* Angus Campbell notes: "Modern Americans would probably have some difficulty defining 'perfect virtue,' but they understand the importance of 'external goods.'" Campbell believes that once we earn enough to meet our daily expenses, our satisfaction depends less on money than on the warmth and intimacy we derive from close relationships.

But anyone who has seen a marriage end is likely to feel that money may offer more security than a relationship can. If we begin to feel that the checks we write get more respect and acceptance than we do, we may learn to trust our banks more than our spouses. Many also learn that money can help us be free of an unhappy relationship and ease adjustment to the end of a marriage. Maintaining control of personal assets may therefore be a priority when we consider second marriage.

Money has additional powerful symbolism. Despite recent changes in social values, pollster Daniel Yankelovich found that money is still "a symbol of social worth . . . the main yardstick Americans use for judging other people's social standing." So we depend upon money not only for its economic power, but for the freedom it gives and for the feelings of self-worth it bestows. For many men, especially, self-worth is determined mostly by net worth. Fraught with so many diverse meanings, money issues can infinitely complicate any marriage, and second marriage is certainly no exception.

People who enter second marriages are more aware that the partnership is as much an economic union as a romantic bond. Most couples plan the economic aspects of their households with at least the same level of care that business people use in planning their commercial efforts. They make decisions about mortgages, consumer debt, education for children, and various forms of insurance, as well as planning for taxes and retirement.

If we have ties to a prior family when we remarry, we face a trio of challenges. We need to develop a new home enterprise by merging two sets of economic resources and probably two earning potentials. We need to continue to meet any existing financial obligations to members of our first families. And we probably want to establish or maintain a measure of economic independence, not only as a buffer against the prospect of another divorce, but also to maintain a sense of self-worth. To achieve these objectives, we need to determine with our new spouses how to handle assets brought to the marriage. We also need to agree how to handle money earned by both partners after marriage.

The recommendations we make here have many legal and tax implications. Before following any of our suggestions, we recommend that you review your plans with an attorney and/or an accountant.

Handling Assets You Already Own

Some remarrying spouses have few assets and therefore feel no need to carefully protect them. Even those with a long list of assets may not be concerned about shielding their wealth. They either believe their new mates would not make unwarranted financial claims if the marriage should end, or they trust the courts to assign a fair share to each partner.

But many people were so unhappy about their last divorce negotiations that their worry approaches paranoia. Those who haggled over who got the dog, the children for Thanksgiving, the IBM stock, the stereo, the newer of the two cars, or the rent-controlled apartment will know what we mean. It's possible that only the calm negotiation of these issues before marriage can allay fears. Some people believe that by negotiating a premarital contract, they can know in advance what they will be giving and receiving during, and possibly after, their new marriage.

Antenuptial agreements can make it easier for apprehensive victims of divorce to marry again. But the very presence of the premarital contract can cast a cloud over the marriage it is intended to protect. When couples enter a marriage with a design for the distribution of their assets if it ends, they will hardly be seen as feeling certain that their new relationship is based on a life-long commitment. In addition, the mechanics of a hard negotiation beforehand could chill the warmest of hearts.

Another disadvantage of antenuptial agreements is their contribution to maintaining inequality. These agreements are usually requested by one partner whose assets far exceed those of the other. The legal contract guarantees that this person will continue to have asset control after the marriage, creating a power imbalance that could undermine the equality of the partnership.

Antenuptial agreements may also have the unintended effect of driving a wedge between new mates and stepchildren. Some people rely on the agreement to guarantee that their children will receive money set aside for them. For example, Robert promised each of his children enough money for college educations and the graduate schools of their choice. When he married Sylvia, he was worried that if their marriage ended, either through divorce or his death, Sylvia might lay claim to his children's education funds. So he asked for and got a premarital contract.

This only complicated the situation. First, Sylvia was hurt by his belief that she would even think of taking money that was meant for the children. She wondered how he could really know her and believe that she could do such a thing. Also, his suspicions did not go unnoticed by his children. He was surprised to find that they became distrustful of Sylvia and guarded in her presence.

Before beginning the negotiation process, Robert should have thought through the potential implications for everyone in the family. In addition, he should have realized that an antenuptial agreement is only one means of protecting the interests of his children. A will would have been a better way to accomplish his objective.

Sociologist Lenore J. Weitzman has noted that the courts have reversed rulings that couples could not enter into a contract before marriage that would control the circumstances of its end. Now the courts treat these contracts as valid legal agreements, as long as they meet the test of traditional contract standards. While spouses may reach agreements concerning property and support, no court has yet ruled that a husband can bargain away his obligation to support his wife *during* the marriage, nor have husbands been permitted to pay their wives a salary for domestic services.

Dr. Weitzman's review of antenuptial contracts revealed that most begin with a statement or purpose of the agreement and go on to specify its duration, prescribe separate ownership of property held by each spouse before their marriage, and shared ownership of property acquired during their marriage. About half of the contracts she studied also included provisions for the drafting of new wills. If the former spouse had been left as executor or administrator of the inheritance, the designation must be changed so that the new spouse is not beholden economically to the former spouse if the marriage should end by death.

The insecurity that might lead one partner to request an antenuptial contract can inspire insecurity in the other. Fear of such a reaction can inhibit some courting couples from raising the issue. Then, either one might decide not to marry because this protection is lacking, or they may enter a relationship without this protection and live defensively ever after.

If you do decide to make a prenuptial agreement, it's important to do it carefully. Because the process of negotiating an antenuptial contract is as psychologically delicate as it is legally complex, it should be approached with considerable tact. The negotiation can almost be guaranteed to go more smoothly if the person with the lower net worth initiates the discussion. Once begun, the partners must be careful not to imply suspicion of the other's intentions.

The spirit of the negotiation should be "soft" rather than "hard." In a soft negotiation, requests are designed to achieve a mutually satisfactory goal. In a hard negotiation, demands are aimed at achieving a victory for one at the other's expense. The strategy of soft negotiators is summarized by the motto, "I can't win if *we* don't both gain something," while hard negotiators contend that "You have to lose if I am to win." Spouses judge one another in terms of the way they bargain, looking for signs of cooperation and fairness. Bargaining strategies aimed toward mutual growth rather than personal gain create cooperation and trust.

Antenuptial agreements can be negotiated through soft bargaining if each person begins by frankly stating his or her objective—e.g., to maintain a measure of economic security at least until the new marriage is tested, or to guarantee protection of any children. The couple should then prepare separate lists of their assets including things like equity in their homes, cash, investments, and personal property. Each should then ask the other for suggestions as to how specific assets can be managed so as to facilitate attainment of a goal. Because sensitivities are acute during such discussions, both partners have an obligation not to read any accusation or threat into the discussion.

If you and your partner decide to have an antenuptial agreement, you may want to make the agreement time-limited. For example, you might agree to gradually transfer your separately held assets to a common marital pot. You may set a goal of making all assets common property within five or ten years, and then specify the amount or percentage to be transferred each year. Another alternative is to agree that all of the income derived from the assets held in separate names will go to the common pot, with the principal remaining separate. You could also protect some but not all of your premarital assets by contributing a portion to the common pot as an act of good faith.

Antenuptial contracts are a powerful force. Some marriages can occur only after this kind of agreement allays financial fears. Other marriages that might have been damaged by a significant and lasting economic imbalance can be facilitated by the creation of an agreement to distribute assets equally over time. But as we have stressed, these pacts can wreak havoc in a second marriage if they are formulated in a sprit of fear and hostility, or if they are poorly conceived. Tact and good advisers are therefore essential if antenuptial agreements are to improve the quality of the marriage they help to create.

Managing Current Income

While antenuptial contracts are not for everyone, all of us need to make decisions about money as soon as we start to share our life with another. We generally make our economic decisions according to one of two models. The "three-pot model" is based on the assumption that partners should have separate as well as shared money. There are three pots: his, hers, and theirs. The couple negotiates the use of money in the common pot, but each partner is free to use private money for any purpose. There are two major variations of the three-pot model:

a. Partners allocate a fixed amount of money or a percentage of income earned by each for personal use, and the rest goes into the common pot. If there is a chance of not being able to cover shared expenses, common obligations are met before individual money is distributed.

b. Partners contribute either a fixed amount or a percentage of what each earns to a common account which contains only what is necessary to cover joint expenses. All remaining money is kept by whoever earned it.

In contrast to the three-pot model which is based in part on the value of independence, the "one-pot model" assumes total interdependence, and views the couple as a single unit. Couples adopting this approach pool all of their resources and use them in ways that are mutually agreeable.

Studies have shown that the three-pot approach is often used in more affluent families where self reliance is highly valued and former spouses are involved in the new marriage. The one-pot model is the more popular choice in families with modest economic resources, an orientation to mutual support, and freedom from active economic involvement with partners or children from prior marriages.

Neither model is necessarily better than the other. Your choice should be based upon your economic situation and your personal needs and values. If you have only enough money to make ends meet, it will almost certainly have to go into a single pot. If you make more than you need to pay the bills, you have the option of using the three-pot approach.

Keeping most of the money jointly can have a valuable symbolic effect, as it represents a high level of trust in each other and belief in the permanence of the relationship. At the same time, having some separate funds can meet a very important need. No one wants to buy birthday presents for a spouse who will inevitably discover the cost, and even possibly question the wisdom of the expense. And we all like to make occasional self-indulgent purchases without having to justify them to our mates. Women who don't have their own discretionary funds sometimes feel so uncomfortable having to account for personal expenditures that they try to save a few dollars from the household money or otherwise disguise payment for the items. This kind of compromising situation can be avoided if each partner has some discretionary funds.

If it is compatible with your tax situation, we suggest the following guidelines for the distribution of money:

a.   agree to keep a modest amount or percentage of your incomes in separate accounts for totally personal uses that need not be discussed;

b.   put the remaining money in a common pot from which current and long-range expenses will be paid.

The decisions about money do not end with its ownership, because there are many choices to be made about how to spend common funds. After marriage, most of us discover differences of opinions about money that we never dreamed would exist. Some cause continual problems while others interfere only when the unexpected occurs.

Many of our erroneous expectations about money management can be traced to the secret contracts we form in courtship. For example, while they were dating Tim took Gwen and her children out for dinner at least twice a week and paid the check without batting an eye. Gwen was not unreasonable in expecting the pattern to continue after they were married. But after Tim became a husband and stepfather, his attitude toward dining out changed. During courtship, he considered it an effective but extravagant way to spend some time with Gwen and give her children a chance to know and like him. But after marriage, he felt the money should be used for more practical purposes. Gwen was annoyed at what she considered Tim's violation of a commitment he had never intended to make.

There is, of course, only one way to avoid misunderstandings like this. Either before you marry, or early in your marriage, you should discuss the use of your shared funds. We do not recommend budgeting, because we have yet to find people who give their budgets more than a passing nod. Junior's broken leg, your sister's third (unexpected) baby, or "in-store specials" on hamburger are the stuff of which inevitable budget-breaking expenditures are made.

Most budgets establish the maximum amount that couples think they should spend for each category of goods or services. The problem with this approach is that we never seem to allocate enough in certain areas, and then once we overspend, we feel it's hopeless, and we stop even trying to budget. But budgeting can provide useful guidelines, and we suggest a minimum budgeting approach. To do this, allocate minimum sums each pay-period to selected areas, being certain that you have a left-over contingency fund. This fund can be used to meet the cost of unexpected opportunity, impulse, or unanticipated need. You won't have any more money available using the minimum approach, but you may find it easier to stay within agreed-upon financial guidelines.

To use any budgeting technique, you must naturally begin by determining just how much after-tax income you have available each month. Then you should list fixed expenses like mortgage payments or rent, insurance, utilities, child support, alimony, and the like. So far, the task is easy because you have relatively little flexibility. The difficulties begin when you need to use personal discretion. We can survive equally well on generic brand foods or gourmet foods. You might want to eat cheaply so as to have more money for entertainment, while your partner might yearn for exotic delicacies, and consider fine dining the only entertainment worth its cost. Therefore, even expenditures for staples like food must be determined by each person's wishes in the context of all the other possible uses of your funds. Be prepared, then, for different personal values to come into play with every budget item you each list.

A Framework for Making Decisions

Rather than arguing over money, you can negotiate a strategy for its use. This negotiation begins by deciding who should have the authority to make the choice. When areas of authority are unclear, too much time is wasted arguing over who has the responsibility and power. And the partner who yields to the other's wishes builds resentment that eventually leads to further argument. This can be avoided through agreeing in advance who will have authority to make decisions.

Two rules are helpful in determining who should make which decisions. First:

The person who will have responsibility to implement the decision should have most of the authority to make the decision.

For example, Rob has been making the investment decisions for his family. Their money has been appreciating, and Nancy has no complaints about Rob's money-management skills. But she has very strong feelings about not wanting to buy stocks in companies that do business with the Department of Defense. So while she is pleased with the growth of their investments, she's unhappy with the source of that growth.

Rob thinks constantly about their portfolio and worries about making poor judgements. He shares Nancy's values, but feels that the need to check out each company's major contracts would be too much work. Therefore he has told Nancy that if she has strong feelings about investments, she can assume the responsibility for making them. She must decide whether making investments her way is worth the effort it would take. If it is a high priority value for her, she should assume control. If it's not important enough, she can ask Rob to consider her preferences, but she should accept his decisions once they are made.

As a second rule:

Couples should reach a balance of decision-making authority that each feels is equitable.

Equity is different from equality: it is a belief that things are fair, while equality suggests a split down the middle. Nancy might feel very strongly about investments and savings, but she might not care at all about how most of the money is spent once investments are made and the other bills are paid. From Nancy's perspective, it may be equitable for Robert to make most of the spending decisions as long as she can have a say in those that are most important to her.

To help establish equity, you should start the following exercise by each deciding how important each issue is to you. Use a star ("*") to indicate which items are very important, a plus ("+") to show which have moderate importance, and a minus ("−") for those with little importance. You will use these symbols later to decide whether you each feel that the authority distribution is equitable.

You can use the following scale to decide who should have authority for making each type of decision.

H	H/w	H/W	W/h	W

H: The husband decides, but offers his wife occasional veto authority.

H/w: The husband decides, but with careful consideration of his wife's opinions and preferences.

H/W: The couple shares decision making authority. In
      some cases they can find a mutually acceptable com-
      promise, and in others they can take turns deciding,
      using the H/w and W/h models in equal balance.

W/h: The wife decides, but with careful consideration of
      her husband's opinions and preferences.

W: The wife decides, but offers her husband occasional
      veto authority.

Proper use of this scale requires some additional explanation. First, note that neither spouse has absolute authority in
any area. When we marry, we exchange independence for
interdependence because every decision made by one partner
can have an impact on the other. The extreme points on the
scale (H and W) represent areas in which you and your
partner make important decisions yourselves, but with the
agreement that you will change your mind if the other expresses very deep concern. These reservations should be very
strong, however, before they are expressed, and you should
each cast only a few of these vetoes over a long period of
time. Given that these vetoes are cast selectively, they should
be heeded if no compromise can be reached.

As an example, one wife cares a great deal about her
clothes, and she spends considerable effort on finding clothes
she likes and can afford. Because her husband has little interest in what she wears, her clothing decisions belong in the
W category (i.e., hers to make with an occasional veto by her
husband). In contrast, her husband is almost indifferent
about the way he dresses; in fact, his wife cares more about
his appearance than he does. In this situation, his clothing
choices should be his own, but open to more frequent comment by his wife (i.e., the H/w category).

The H/w and W/h categories allow more room for continuing discussion and compromise. Either spouse can express a preference and the other can ask for something differ-

ent. You should always try to find a mutually satisfactory resolution, but the person who has the responsibility for carrying out the decision has the right to make the final decision.

For example, a wife has been driving the same car for 12 years. The car even has a name and has been a steady, reliable friend for her. Now the engine needs a $400 overhaul, and since this couple uses a one-pot model, large expenditures must be decided mutually. She would like to spend the money to keep the car, but her husband wants her to trade it for a new one. He believes that a new car would be much safer and less expensive to maintain, while she claims that the money would be wisely and reasonably spent to maintain her old car. Who should have the authority to make the decision?

The wife has to drive the car every day, and she is the one who will have to deal with the effects of an accident should one occur. But large expenditures are of mutual concern, and furthermore, her husband would be affected by any injury to his wife. This decision should probably be in the W/h category; her decision to make, but one in which she gives careful consideration to her husband's desires.

The third decision-making category is generally used to resolve issues about which both partners have strong feelings and fairly equal responsibility. In these situations, you should negotiate until you reach a mutually satisfactory decision. Sometimes, you will be able to reach a compromise or choice agreeable to both. Other times, you will decide to let one person make the decision in exchange for an agreement that the other can make the decision next time.

This category often includes a wide range of decisions of varying importance. At one end are issues like whether to spend entertainment money on concert tickets or records. In the middle range are decisions like whether to use vacation time to go skiing or visit friends. All of these decisions can usually be made by finding a mutually satisfying choice or taking turns doing what each person likes best.

Larger issues, like whether to buy a house or move into a larger apartment, pose greater challenge. This decision will hinge on considerations like who is willing to assume how much financial responsibility and how the move would affect each partners' commutes to work. Decisions in these areas of great importance to both are best made on the basis of the best possible mutual satisfaction, with some deference to the partner who will have the greater responsibility.

Now that we have described and illustrated each category, we would like to offer a few guidelines to make agreement as easy as possible.

1.   If only one person feels very strongly about a particular issue and accepts responsibility for taking the necessary action, the decision should be in the H or W category. If the person without responsibility wants some authority, you can use the H/w or W/h categories, perhaps with an agreement to share some of the responsibility.

2.   If partners have equally strong or weak feelings about a particular item, the one who will have the greater responsibility for taking the necessary action should have most of the authority. Either the H/w or W/h category should be used.

3.   If both partners are equally interested or disinterested in an item, and if they have equal responsibility for implementation, they can assign it to the H/W category.

As your negotiation progresses, remember the importance of equity as opposed to equality. Allowing each person to have a strong voice in areas he or she considers important is more valuable than arriving at a balanced number of areas in each category.

This decision-making framework is a start. Any time your circumstances change, you may have to renegotiate some of your decisions. When you win the state lottery and have endless piles of hundred dollar bills, you won't have to worry about who decides how to spend money, because you'll never spend it all. When you both retire and your income goes

MONEY: AUTHORITY AND RESPONSIBILITY

Area	Importance *, +, −	Authority H,Hw,HW,Wh,W
Housing		
Home decoration		
Entertainment equipment		
Home repair		
Appliances		
Husband's car		
Wife's car		
Car repairs		
Husband's clothes		
Wife's clothes		
Husband's personal expenses		
Wife's personal expenses		
Food		
Household expenses		
Money for husband's parents, relatives		
Money for wife's parents, relatives		
Vacations		

Area	Importance	Authority
Entertainment		
Dining out		
Church contributions		
Contributions to political parties		
Contributions to charities		
Savings account		
"Safe" investments		
"Growth" investments		
Children's allowance		
Children's education		
Extra education for husband		
Extra education for wife		
Payments on husband's old debts (school, car, child support)		
Payments on wife's old debts (school, car, child support)		
Payments on shared debts		
Other		

down sharply, you may have to develop some new priorities. Each time either partner feels unhappy with the current agreement, return to this framework and negotiate a new distribution of authority.

We have recommended a process for making decisions about money, but we've left the content up to you. The priorities attached to the use of money are very personal, and depend on each couple's income, needs, and desires. However you slice the economic pie, you should do everything possible to assure that you both can depend on receiving your fair share.

6
Understanding Each Other

"My wife just didn't understand me."
"My husband could never see my point of view."

By the time a first marriage breaks up, nearly everyone feels misunderstood. And if the truth be known, most remarried partners have an occasional sense of *déjà vu* with a second spouse. Despite the best intentions, faulty communication often gets in the way of understanding. Not only does it interfere with the sharing of innermost feelings, but it even creates confusion in determining such seemingly simple things as who had agreed to drive the kids home from school or who would prepare dinner.

When we run into familiar communication problems in our second marriages, we may start to doubt our ability to choose an appropriate mate. We may even wonder whether men and women can ever truly understand one another. The problem lies not so much in mate selection or sex differences, however, but in the fact that communication is extremely complex and not easily done well. Although there is never a time in our lives when we are not communicating, practice seldom leads to perfection.

When we think about communication, we usually consider only spoken words. But the manner in which things are said, including voice tone, eye contact, and gestures, reveals more of the message than words ever convey. And actions, or even lack of action, are even more powerful than spoken messages.

For example, Paul and Sandra often accused each other of saying things that the other denied having ever said. One common argument centered on the treatment of their children from their previous marriages. Sandra felt that Paul didn't like her children, and Paul felt that Sandra was indifferent to his. Both felt falsely accused, because each had deliberately avoided making negative comments about the other's children. Neither realized that their attitudes were conveyed in many indirect and unintentional non-verbal ways. Paul would sometimes physically withdraw when his stepdaughter tried to give him a kiss or a hug. Sandra often managed to have pressing work commitments when her stepson was playing in a Little League game. While they paid lip-service to loving each other's kids, each perceived the "real" message in the nonverbal behavior, and they gave little credence to the spoken word. *Whenever there is a conflict between what is said and what is done, the words will be ignored and the actions will be taken as truth.*

Paul and Sandra each thought they only communicated the things they intended to express. But communication is any behavior that carries a message perceived by someone else. It is inherent in virtually everything we do (e.g., call home) or don't do (e.g., "forget" to call); and everything we say (e.g., "I love you") or don't say (e.g., silence in response to the question "Do you love me?"). And we communicate whether or not we intend to do so. *Since we cannot NOT behave, we cannot NOT communicate.*

Many of the functions of communication are obvious, such as crying for help, warning of danger, bargaining for the things we want, or simply passing the time of day. But often present in the messages we send is a hidden request for approval from our listener. The information we receive helps to build our personal identity; without feedback from others we cannot possibly build a good sense of who we are.

From infancy on, we are aware of the way others react to us, and we use their reactions to help form our beliefs about ourselves. If we receive approval, we feel good about ourselves; if we are criticized, we feel rejected. Information from others also provides us with the form and color that fill in the details of our identity.

In a very real sense, we think of ourselves as the kind of people we believe other people think we are. We feel intelligent or stupid, interesting or boring, attractive or unappealing according to our perceptions of the way others react to us. Since we are always getting feedback (behavior equals communication equals feedback), our self images are constantly being affirmed or challenged. The more consistent the messages from others, the more consistent our self images will be.

The need to protect and enhance our self-concept is so strong that it influences every aspect of our communication. We are selective about what we say to other people because we want them to think well of us. We only reveal negative things about ourselves to those we trust to like us despite their knowledge of our flaws.

For a husband and wife, the messages they exchange with each other are far more important than those they exchange with anyone else. We usually reveal our most intimate thoughts to our mates, and we trust them to use what they hear to help us feel good about ourselves. We want our partners to be candid in responding to our self disclosures, but we feel understood only when the candor takes the form of approval.

Although we constantly seek our mate's approval, we usually try to get it *in*directly. For example, when Paul told Sandra that he bought new snow tires at the Labor Day sale, he wanted to do more than simply convey information; he also wanted recognition and approval. Paul wanted Sandra to notice how clever he was for thinking ahead, how thrifty for taking advantage of a prewinter sale, and how considerate for buying the tires so she wouldn't have to bother. When Sandra responded by asking if new tires were really necessary, Paul felt she was telling him that he was foolish and wasteful to have spent the money, and inconsiderate for not consulting with her first. As is so often true, what appeared to be a inconsequential exchange had deep and far-reaching implications. Self-esteem was the major issue in the snow tire discussion, just as it is in most conversations between husbands and wives.

When people don't respond to our requests for recognition and approval, we feel slighted. When others disagree with us, we may feel rejected. We often act as if the core of our identity is symbolized by every one of our words and deeds.

At the merest hint of the other's disinterest or disapproval, we are likely to respond with reflexive insecurity and defensiveness. This desire to protect ourselves affects not only what we say, but also what we hear and remember in every conversation. We seek information that supports our attitudes and beliefs and and we either fail to hear or don't recall anything that contradicts them.

When our marriages go well, we hear approving and supportive messages whether or not they exist. But in times of stress, we are very keenly sensitive to the merest hint of rejection.

When Paul married Sandra, he moved into the house she once shared with her former husband. He wasn't particularly comfortable living there, but her children didn't want to move, and both Paul and Sandra wanted to make the transition easy for the kids. Still, Paul sometimes felt like an intruder, and he never really felt at home.

Paul brought only a few pieces of furniture to Sandra's house, but he brought many boxes of books. When he moved in, he rearranged every book in the house, replacing many of Sandra's books with his own, and storing many of hers in the basement. He knew that he would feel more at home surrounded by the books he regarded as old friends. One day, when Sandra couldn't find a book she needed, she innocently asked Paul if he knew where it was. Paul, ever sensitive to his position as intruder, thought he detected annoyance in her voice. His reaction was defensive and angry, spurred by the feeling that she resented even the minor ways he tried to make himself at home in *her* house. It would have been so much simpler if he just accepted her question at face value rather than hearing it as an accusation.

Paul made a listening and interpretative error, the kind we all make all too often. Because we are exposed to thousands of stimuli every second, we must filter most of them out. If we tried to weigh each detail individually, we would spend a year trying to make sense of every minute. In addition to filtering, we also quickly classify our impressions into familiar categories. We stay attentive until any hint tells us that this experience is similar to one we had before. Then, whether or not the present and past situations have anything in common, we act as if they do. That's one way we help the past repeat itself.

Because we do so much filtering and filling in of details, we always act on incomplete and biased information. Since each person experiences every event differently, it is to be expected that we will disagree about who holds the "right" view. Whether the difference is between nations or mates, a successful resolution is impossible as long as each side tries to enlighten the other about the "truth." Even if such an essence exists, neither side can ever know it.

Our "perceptions" are always biased by a large element of self deception. We all act as if we know what's taking place around us, but at best we can only think we know. Any time we argue over facts, we are actually fighting over the different ways we think the "facts" should be interpreted.

In order to better understand the subjective nature of most communication, it helps to distinguish between "hard" and "soft" meanings. "Hard" meanings apply to objects that are objectively measurable, such as "chair," or to very solid concepts, such as "student" or "grandfather." "Soft" meanings are much harder to define, and involve those entirely personal, individual, and subjective judgments about the things we think we see.

In many ways, soft meanings are the core concepts around which we organize our lives. Words like "respectful," "honorable," "sensitive," and "loving" have only soft meanings. Many of the arguments between spouses focus on these very personal interpretations. For example, Paul agreed to accompany his ex-wife to their daughter's graduation, at the child's request. He believed he was being "mature" and "considerate" for setting aside his bad feelings about his wife for the sake of their child. Sandra, on the other hand, felt that by appearing in public with his ex-wife, he was being "disloyal" to her and "inconsiderate" of her feelings.

We have to be very careful about using negative trait descriptions. Like all descriptions, they are based on selective and biased perceptions of the way other people behave. Once we conclude that a person is "untrustworthy," "unkind," or "self-absorbed," we tend to act as if these were absolute truths with hard instead of soft meanings. These are almost always conclusions that are too harsh and too rigidly accepted.

Negative trait words are too harsh because we all act differently according to the situation. For example, Paul felt responsible for accompanying his ex-wife to the graduation, but he certainly did not want to spend social time with her. Negative trait judgments are also unfair because they often involve predictions about the behavior of others based on our —not their—past experience. For example, Sandra's first husband left her for another woman, and she worried that Paul could do the same. Unfortunately, Sandra has not been able to set her past experience aside. Instead, she looks for hints of infidelity in everything Paul does.

The confusion between objective and subjective perception arises in part from our tendency to assume that anything that can be described in words is an objective fact. In his book *Crazy Talk, Stupid Talk,* Neil Postman clarifies this concept by explaining the "is" of projection. When we say "He *is* stupid," we create the impression that stupidity can be objectively determined, like eye color. But whether any act is considered smart or stupid is dependent on the way varied observers assess its circumstances and its end result.

We habitually confuse words with things; we respond to words as if they are the things they symbolize. As a result, *we often forget that others may honestly see things differently, and their view is as true for them as ours is for us.*

Why do we assume that our perceptions are facts? Because life moves at a fast pace and there isn't time to gather and carefully evaluate all the information we receive. We learn instead to make a few observations, infer the rest, and act as though we knew *the truth.* If we were fully aware that all perceptions are subjective, we might be paralyzed by indecision. Treating our selective perceptions and personal interpretations as fact enables us to act.

Simplifying communication is difficult because all messages are sent and received on two levels, content and context. The content is whatever is overtly said or done. This can best be determined by an independent, unbiased observer. The context provides directions for interpreting the overt message. The context includes the history of the relationship, the current feelings of both of the speakers, the situation in which the communication is taking place, and dozens of nonverbal behaviors. In their insightful book *Pragmatics of Human Communication,* Watzlawick, Beavin-Bavelas, and Jackson observed that content "remains unexplainable as long as the range of observation is not wide enough to include the context in which the phenomenon occurs."

Even in the intimacy of marital communication, each person depends upon a different context to help in understanding anything that takes place. For example, "I'm exhausted" means "I'd like some appreciation for how hard I work" to Paul. But when Sandra's first husband complained about fatigue, he was saying: "No sex tonight." So whenever Paul complains of being tired, Sandra becomes tense and withdrawn. Paul's bid for contact thus becomes Sandra's cue for greater distance. Both are left confused and hurt because of their failure to understand the context each uses to interpret what is said and done.

Context provides directions for interpretation. These directions are seldom made explicit, but they are always present and always a comment on the relationship itself. Because these relationship-defining instructions are subject to soft interpretation, we must be prepared for occasional disagreements. We can argue endlessly about what someone "really" said, when in fact, there are two equally "real" messages:

a.   what the speaker *thinks* is said; and
b.   what the listener *thinks* is said.

Because the actual words spoken are such a small part of any message, discussion of content is almost irrelevent. Only an exchange of interpretations can yield fruitful results.

The following example of communication as an exchange of interpretations will illustrate the complexity of even an apparently simple interchange. Sandra had this conversation with Herb, her first husband, shortly before their marriage ended. They had just had a brief chat with an acquaintance who told them about her new job.

SANDRA: Her work sounds so boring and useless.
HERB: I think it sounds interesting. Why do you have to judge her?
SANDRA: If she likes it, that's fine. I'm just saying that I could never do that kind of work.
HERB: I don't think your work is any more noble than hers.
SANDRA: Maybe you should find yourself someone whose work you respect!
HERB: Maybe I should.

This conversation was the beginning of a major fight, after which both Sandra and Herb felt hurt, rejected, and angry.

Neither could understand why the other had been so judgmental and unreasonable, yet each "knew" that the other was being very critical. If they had been able to view their interaction on the context level instead of the content level, they would have been aware of the following very important details:

History: Herb feels that Sandra disapproves of people like him who work for large corporations. Sandra feels that Herb wants her to get a job that will pay more than she now earns as a social worker. Both Herb and Sandra love their work and are angry at the lack of support they get from the other.

Situation: They have just conversed with a friend who was describing her well-paying job in advertising.

>*(She thinks: "I bet he wishes I had a job like that.")*
> She says: "Her work sounds so boring and useless."

>*(He thinks: "There she goes criticizing business people again. I know she thinks my job is useless, too.")*
> He says: "I think it sounds interesting. What right do you have to judge her?"

>*(She thinks: "Now I'm being accused of being judgmental. As if I care what this woman does for a living!")*
> She says: "If she likes it, that's fine. I'm just saying that I could never do that kind of work."

>*(He thinks: "Oh, so it's fine for people like me, but she's too good for it! As if what she does for a living is so valuable.")*
> He says: "I don't think your work is any more noble than hers."

>*(She thinks: "So he thinks my work is useless! And I thought he respected my profession! I wonder what other judgments he's making of me? He doesn't understand me at all!")*
> She says: "Maybe you should find yourself someone whose work you respect!"

*(He thinks: "She doesn't care if I stay or go. Well, I
know someone who will appreciate me.")*
He says: "Maybe I should."

Notice how quickly the content changes from discussion of
their friend's new job to finding new and more appreciative
partners. All the important communicating was about the
relationship, although this was not made explicit until both
were too angry to discuss it.

What is important in this interchange is not the language
itself but the way words are used to convey each person's
perception. Since every message expresses something about
the relationship between speaker and listener, an awareness
of this relationship-defining level is crucial.

Most of us rely on nonverbal behavior as one way to peek
behind the veil of spoken words. Voice tone, eye contact,
facial expression, body position, and many other nonverbal
cues are indicators of the "real" message being conveyed. We
all learn to trust these cues because nonverbal behaviors are
harder to manipulate and therefore a more accurate expression of our feelings.

Nonverbal behavior is particularly revealing in intimate
communication. As a test, you might try saying "I love you"
using four different tones of voice that would change its
meaning from deep love to sarcasm or indifference. Then
choose the tone that sounds most sincere to you, and, standing before a mirror, change eye contact, facial expression,
and body position to vary the meaning from a genuine statement of love to an insincere or angry gesture. You'll discover
that even when your voice tone is most sincere, you can
weaken the meaning of your words by changing other nonverbal cues.

Sometimes when we feel misunderstood by our mates, they
are attending to nonverbal cues beyond our awareness. For
example, one morning Sandra came into the kitchen and
found Paul absorbed in the sports section of the newspaper.
In response to her "Good morning," he wished her a good
morning without looking up. Sandra, interpreting his re-

sponse to mean that batting averages were more important to him than she was, silently prepared breakfast for herself, deliberately banging some pots and knocking a few dishes together in the process. Paul realized that she was angry, but he didn't know why.

An argument developed in which each accused the other of being distant and rejecting. Both felt unjustly punished, since they saw themselves as having done nothing more than simply try to start the day pleasantly while the other clearly communicated rejection in nonverbal ways.

Because there is a relationship-defining aspect to every verbal and nonverbal exchange between intimates, we are often quick to take offense at anything that might indicate lack of respect or caring. The most common negative nonverbal communications in marriage occur when a presumed lack of consideration is interpreted by the other to mean "what you think and feel doesn't matter to me."

We can't prevent all misinterpretations, but we can reduce their frequency. First, we must acknowledge the complexity of communication and the need to refine our communication skills. Then, we can learn specific techniques to help make it more likely that the messages sent are the messages received.

Listening

Many of us often act as if listening involves nothing more than staying silent while another person talks. Instead of thinking about what's being said, we silently rehearse what we plan to say as soon the speaker pauses for a breath. Often, the speech of others seems like little more than a tedious interruption of our own expression of ideas.

Even when we try to concentrate on what others are saying, we are more likely to judge than understand. Feeling sure that we know their intentions, we see no need to ask "What do you mean?" and instead we ask ourselves "Is that right or wrong?" Since we often pay closer attention to what we think than to what the speaker says, our reaction can leave the other person feeling misunderstood and frustrated.

Good listeners are *active* listeners. To set the stage for active listening, we must curb our tendency to hear only the words, to judge without asking questions, or to gather only enough details to allow us to plan our own response. We can't assume that everyone thinks the way we do, or means what we would have meant had we said the same things.

There is only one way to understand another person's perspective: *Ask!* To be good listeners, we have to do some talking. We should gather information by asking questions about what the speaker is saying. Then we should check out our interpretations by asking the speaker whether what we thought we heard is what the speaker intended to communicate.

Before illustrating good listening techniques, let's start with an example of poor listening. In this vignette, a husband has arrived home an hour late to find his wife waiting for him. Both are visibly upset.

GREG: What a day I had!

JILL: You think you've had a bad day! I had to leave work early because the kids wouldn't stop calling me to complain about each other.

GREG: The kids are always fighting. It's no big deal. My boss is putting so much pressure on me that I don't know if I can stand it much longer.

JILL: I thought Josh was going to break Sarah's arm. I'm really worried about his temper.

GREG: If you want to know about bad temper, try working with my boss. I need to get transferred to another department.

JILL: You can't think about anything but work. Don't you even care about your own children?

GREG: That's just great. My boss thinks I'm a lousy worker and you think I'm a lousy father. I don't know why I even bother to try.

It's easy to imagine the kind of fight that can develop from this exchange. Both partners are so wrapped up in their own concerns that they can't listen to each other. The discussion quickly goes from a content-focus to a relationship-focus where each feels victimized by the other's lack of understanding.

The use of good listening techniques could have prevented this argument. Here is one way that Jill could have responded differently:

GREG: What a day I had!

JILL: I figured something was wrong when you weren't home at six. What happened?

GREG: My boss is putting a lot of pressure on me. I don't know what I'm going to do.

JILL: You sound really upset. What kind of pressure is he putting on you?

GREG: He wants me to live at work. I just can't do it, and I'm afraid of what might happen.

JILL: Are you afraid of being fired?

GREG: Sometimes I worry about that.

Instead of countering Greg's expression of distress with her own, Jill asks questions ("What happened?". . ." What kind of pressure is he putting on you?") that allow her to get more information about why Greg is upset. She also does some reflection of feelings ("You sound really upset.") which enables him to know that she understands his feelings as well as his words. Finally, she checks her own understanding of what he is saying by asking if he is afraid that he might lose his job. Once Jill feels she has a fairly good understanding of Greg's concerns, and Greg has had a fair hearing, it would be her turn to voice her concerns, and Greg's turn to actively listen.

The initial conversation could have just as easily been altered by Greg. Here is how he could have used good listening skills:

GREG: What a day I had!

JILL: You think you had a horrible day! I had to leave work early because the kids wouldn't stop fighting.

GREG: It looks like we're going to have a lot to talk about tonight. Why don't you start by telling me what happened with the kids?

JILL: I thought Josh was going to break Sarah's arm.

GREG: That really is frightening. What exactly did he do?

JILL: She was annoying him in some way, and he grabbed her arm and twisted it behind her back.

GREG: So his response was way out of line with what she did to provoke him?

JILL: Yeah, he really overreacted.

Here, Greg is taking responsibility for asking questions ("Why don't you start by telling me what happened with the kids?" "What exactly did he do?") and reflecting feelings ("That really is frightening."). He also paraphrases ("So his response was way out of line . . .") in order to make sure that the message sent is the message received.

In both examples of good listening, each partner asked two questions near the beginning of the conversation. It is helpful to follow the *"two-question rule"* in which the answer to an initial question is followed by a second question based on the answer. Here is what could have happened if Greg had only asked one question of Jill:

"Why don't you tell me what happened with the kids?"

"I was afraid that Josh was going to break Sarah's arm."

"I'd like to break both of my bosses arms!"

Because it's so easy and natural for us to respond to what others say by relating it to ourselves, the *two-question rule* helps us keep the focus on the other person. Only when we listen with a minimum of projection or self-reference can we start to truly understand other people.

Why do we use the *two-question rule* so seldom? Because most conversations are contests between two speakers struggling to gain and hold the floor. We seem to be afraid that if we're not the first to speak, we'll lose the chance entirely. As illustrated by Greg and Jill, the person who speaks first feels as though the other ignored what was said. So the second speaker's response is ignored as the first speaker makes another attempt to be heard. Just as two people speaking different languages raise their voices in response to the frustration of not being understood, two people who feel ignored make their own points with increasing vigor.

Instead of competing for the position of first speaker, we can improve our communication and increase our feelings of intimacy by vying to be first listener. When we begin conversations by showing our partners that we are eager to understand their thoughts and feelings, they are likely to do the same.

Acceptance

Anyone who has been divorced knows how a bad relationship can erode feelings of self-worth. Even if we felt understood, we couldn't be happy unless we felt accepted. We depend upon our partners to keep us feeling good about ourselves and our relationship.

To appreciate the importance of acceptance, we should remember that we constantly seek approval from those we love and respect. When we feel that our thoughts, feelings, or opinions are not respected by those whose opinions matter, our defenses go up and productive conversation is almost impossible. Once threatened, our energy is diverted from understanding to defensiveness. We can increase our awareness of the other person's point of view, and have true understanding, only when there is mutual trust.

No matter how carefully we try to listen, some misunderstanding is inevitable. The feeling of acceptance that we convey offers some compensation for the frustration of being misinterpreted. So acceptance and respect are not only necessary prerequisites to good listening, they also soften the impact of the imprecision in even the best of listening.

What are some of the ways in which we habitually fail to convey respect and caring for each other? Sometimes we put each other down by labeling or name-calling. At other times, we'll hear our partners' opinions, but never allow ourselves to be influenced by them. And we use nonverbal behaviors that show a lack of interest, like reading the paper while "listening." All of these make it easy for our spouses to feel we don't care.

Most of the problems in our first marriages can be traced to a basic feeling of not being valued and appreciated. Many of us can describe obvious ways in which we felt our former spouses put us down. We may have felt victimized by verbal or physical abuse, extreme neglect, or extramarital affairs. More often, however, our unhappiness resulted from the gradual accumulation of small instances of misunderstanding, lack of appreciation, and disrespect. Because happiness can slowly erode through small careless acts, couples in the best of second marriages still need to assure that each partner consistently feels valued and respected.

Like listening, the process of affirming the worth of another person is really quite simple. We must always convey respect for our partners' opinions, regardless of whether or not we agree. When our spouses seem to be acting irrationally, we must assume that from their own points of view, the reactions make sense. Our task, then, is to learn more about that point of view by using good listening techniques.

Here is an example of how a poor response can lead to trouble.

PETER: My kids are coming by to pick up some books, so I asked them to stay for dinner.

NORA: Since I do the cooking, you shouldn't ask anyone to dinner without my O.K.

Even if Nora is correct and Peter didn't consider her feelings, her response has put him on the defensive. Instead of reaching an agreement about how and when Peter will invite his children for dinner, they will argue over whether

Peter was thoughtless or Nora too rigid. In defending them-selves against both real and imagined accusations, they won't let down their guard enough to see each other's point of view.

Regardless of her feelings about Peter's invitation, Nora had a choice: she could vent her feelings or she could try to solve the problem. As we've seen, venting feelings results in defensive counter-accusations. She could have gotten a con-structive response by offering a positive interpretation of his behavior followed by a request for change. For example, she could have said:

NORA: I'm glad you're spending time with your children, and I don't mind having them over for dinner. But because I never know how much food to buy and prepare, I wish you'd check with me first.

The positive observation would have stimulated Peter's at-tentiveness, and minimized his defensiveness. Once he feels understood and appreciated, he will be more likely to listen to her point of view.

Written words can't convey the importance of the nonver-bal cues that are part of every conversation. If the positive response suggested above was said sarcastically, or while slamming cupboard doors, Peter would still feel put down.

Second marriages provide many opportunities to feel inse-cure. Second spouses often privately compare themselves with their predecessors, and they may be especially sensitive to any implication by their spouses that they don't measure up. Those who have been hurt in a first marriage are likely to be oversensitive to any hint of criticism or rejection. Step-parents may feel rejected by children who make it clear that their loyalty will always be with their natural parents, and they may be hurt when the children fail to express apprecia-tion for acts of kindness. Therefore, partners in second mar-riages must be especially careful to give each other ample amounts of support, understanding, and reassurance.

Straightforwardness

Whenever we take a stand, we risk rejection. We might say something stupid, and lose our mates' respect. We might reveal too much, and become too vulnerable. Or we might be cruel, and prompt our mates' retaliation. Any negative reaction makes us uncomfortable, and we often resort to indirect expression to avoid criticism or rejection.

We use indirect expression when we try to get a message across without facing the risk of being challenged. There are a number of ways in which we can express ourselves indirectly and then deny what we said if we sense disagreement.

A common ploy is to express ourselves nonverbally but deny our message in words. For example, we can display unhappiness by sulking or withdrawing, but when asked why we're upset, we can protest "Why do you think something's wrong? I didn't say a thing." We can also use nonverbal behavior to contradict what we say. For example, if we feel pressured to do something we don't want to do, we can say "That sounds fine," in a dull, flat voice that clearly conveys our lack of enthusiasm. If challenged, we can always retort "I *said* it sounds fine," thereby making matters worse.

Another technique is to project our thoughts and feelings onto our mates. For example, if a new stepparent feels that his partner's children are ungrateful, he might say, "You must feel that the kids are pretty ungrateful at times." If he is then accused of having those feelings himself, he can defend himself by saying "I was only thinking about you," or "You're angry at me because I want to make sure you feel appreciated?" Again, constructive discussion is hardly likely.

We can also use the opinions of other people to make our point. If, for example, a wife feels that her husband is manipulated by his ex-wife, she might say "Our friends think you let your ex push you around too much." Should he accuse her of criticising him, she can reply "I'm just telling you what our friends said," and each will feel unfairly judged.

We express ourselves indirectly to avoid rejection and conflict, but the frustration and anger that result usually bring about exactly what we want to avoid. In addition, indirectly expressed opinions can't earn for us the agreement, sympathy, or understanding that we seek. We can only know and understand each other if we are honest about what we feel.

Having already given examples of what not to do, let's look at some positive guidelines for expressing ourselves straightforwardly.

1. Put negative feelings into words rather than acting them out. Positive feelings can be stated both verbally and nonverbally.
2. Use "I" when making statements about your thoughts or feelings. This clearly shows that the opinions are your own, and not those of your spouse or friends.
3. State your thoughts directly and honestly, but only if you can also meet the requirements of tact and consideration.

With a little practice, the first two guidelines aren't difficult to follow. But we all have to work at tempering directness with tact.

In the attempt to communicate directly and openly, we sometimes do it without considering the feelings of others. Several years ago, it was particularly fashionable for people to say whatever was on their minds. But, as Neil Postman points out, ". . . getting in touch with your feelings [this way] often amounts to losing touch with the feelings of others." And once we've put others on the defensive, we may as well be talking to ourselves.

The complexities of remarriage often breed resentment, and we need to find nonthreatening alternatives to direct statements of resentment. Instead of saying "Because of your kids, we never have time alone together," the stepparent might say "I'd like to spend a little time alone with you. Can we figure out some times when we can be together?" This allows for a direct expression of the desire to spend time without the children, but in a way that doesn't make the parent feel accused or attacked.

If we take the time to put ourselves in our mates' position, we can usually find a tactful way to express our feelings. But if we feel forced to choose between directness and consideration, consideration is the wisest choice.

One way to effectively combine directness with courtesy is to remember that *honesty of intent is more important that honesty of fact.* Some people believe that to be honest, one must tell all, revealing every thought, feeling, and fantasy, regardless of the effect. But a less extreme definition of honesty is more practical. We can concentrate on the honest reporting of actions, but not the reporting of each thought or feeling.

Studies of the relationship between honesty and marital satisfaction reveal that uncensored, open communication may be more than any relationship can bear. There's a little of "the princess and the pea" in all of us. We tend to be hurt by negative messages, even if they are softened by many positives.

When spouses convey too many trivial negative thoughts and feelings, the relationship is likely to suffer. Therefore, we should think carefully before communicating negatives. It helps to ask ourselves "By raising this issue, will I accomplish enough change to risk upsetting my partner?" More often than not we'll conclude that expressing a negative will do more harm than good.

This recommendation of editing or censoring is not an endorsement of lying or "evading the truth." There is no excuse for active deception or concealment. Rather, each partner needs to make many difficult decisions each day about which things are appropriate to say, and which are best left unspoken. When the concealment of facts might lead to a misinterpretation of intent, keeping silent can't be justified. But when concealment does not lead to incorrect conclusions, and if it is done to show consideration rather than to manipulate, it may be acceptable.

For example, it's tactful for a wife not to tell her second husband that she still thinks about some of the good times she had in her first marriage. Regardless of its truth, the statement can only upset him. On the other hand, it is manipulative of her to conceal the fact that she sometimes has long lunches with her ex-husband that are as much for pleasure as for business. In the first instance, the wife used discretion to protect her husband's feelings, while in the second, she withheld information he had a right to know.

When it's hard to decide whether to conceal or reveal, the answer to one question will usually help to solve the problem. Realizing that you and your spouse are two different people, ask yourself what you would want if the situation were reversed and your spouse were trying to decide what to share with you. This can help guard against our tendency to hold ourselves to a lower standard of honesty than we demand from our partner.

Listening, accepting, and tactful straightforwardness are the keys to better communication. Through careful effort, we can steadily improve our ability to understand each other. And as understanding grows, our marriages become stronger, happier, and more secure. But the process is not always easy, and despite our best efforts, few of us can create a totally harmonious relationship. The next chapter will include ways to deal with the conflict that arises in even the best of marriages.

7
Conflict:
Making It Work for You

The only way to avoid conflict in marriage is to stay single. When you are alone, you are with someone who wants exactly what you want when you want it, who can always understand what you mean without need for explanation, and who always has your best interest at heart. But marriage offers rewards seldom found in single life, and part of the price is a certain amount of conflict.

Conflict is certainly no stranger to people in second marriages. They are usually veterans of unhappy first marriages and unpleasant divorces. Second marriages, though happier, create a new set of issues over which to fight. There are disagreements about whose paintings go on the wall and whose go in the closet, jealousies about past spouses, hassles over how to manage his, her, or their children, and many other concerns ranging from the trivial to the fundamental.

No marriage is conflict-free. In many good marriages, the level of satisfaction is about as high as the level of conflict.

It has even been suggested that married people fight *because* of their commitment, not in spite of it.

Why are we so willing to do battle with our spouses? First, and most obvious, we spend more time with our spouses in more varied activities. That gives us many opportunities to disagree. The depth of contact also exposes the messages we exchange to many different levels of meaning. For instance, when a man's friends invite him out for dinner, he hears a simple invitation based on the pleasure of his company. When his wife suggests going out for dinner, he may not be sure what she is really saying. Is she asking for his company away from the children or criticizing him for not offering to take her out often enough?

In addition, we expect more support from our spouses than from anyone else. When we hear actual or implied criticism, the jabs hurt all the more because they are thrown by the person we trust the most. Our romantic notions about marriage often include expectations of total harmony, and are tarnished by signs of marital stress.

Married couples can fight about anything, and usually do. Although most marital arguments focus on money, relatives, and children, many bitter fights erupt over what seems to be nothing at all. Most of us can recall, with some embarrassment, arguments over what to watch on TV or what color to paint the bathroom. One couple recently described a major battle over whether to make tacos or hamburgers for dinner!

Why do we engage in such serious conflict over such trivial matters? *Underlying most arguments is one simple concern: My partner doesn't give me enough love, respect, or caring.* We are seldom aware of this underlying issue because it involves our deepest feelings about ourselves, our marriages, and our beliefs about our partners' perceptions of both. Even if we are aware of these feelings, we may be afraid or reluctant to openly discuss our fears about ourselves or the relationship. We fight over money, TV, or hamburgers, when we are really concerned with the implications for the relationship. As described in the previous chapter, the important meanings often lie in the context rather than the content of a conversation.

Most marital conflicts involve the issue of autonomy (or separateness) vs. mutuality (or connectedness). The challenge of forming a unity of two people without sacrificing either person's individuality is not an easy one to meet. When we feel that our spouses are too controlling or demanding, we fear we may become overpowered and lose part of ourselves. When we feel that our spouses are indifferent, uncaring, or too independent, we may fear losing the relationship.

Conflict is therefore a normal byproduct of the complications that arise any time two people try to function both as a unified couple and as separate individuals. Total elimination of conflicts over autonomy and security is probably impossible. But by openly acknowledging the underlying issues in an argument, we take the first step toward understanding the fights that so often interfere with marital happiness.

Because we are clever at concealing underlying issues even from ourselves, we must first learn to recognize them. The most obvious warning occurs any time our emotional reactions seem out of proportion to the problem at hand. When we recognize that we're overreacting, it's worth asking ourselves whether there might be another, more important concern that deserves our attention. Remember that the underlying question is usually "Do I feel my partner is not showing enough caring, love, or respect?"

Another sign of hidden issues is either partner's use of dirty fighting techniques like rejection and coercion. When the relationship is at issue, we spend less time talking about the specified problem than in calling each other names or forcing our point of view. Any time we feel our identity or our marriage is at stake, we will use attacking and defensive fighting tactics, even though they make the conflict worse.

Finally, any time an argument can't be resolved through

a rational process of understanding or negotiation, deeper, unnamed issues are usually at stake.

When spouses uncover their underlying concerns, they almost always discover that their fears are complementary. For example, if a husband is worried that his wife is too independent and might leave him, she is likely to be equally concerned about being too controlled by her husband. If a wife feels her husband is indifferent and she often tries to get him to pay more attention to her, her husband probably feels that she is too demanding and doesn't allow him the freedom he wants.

Not all conflict, however, is the result of personal fears and defensiveness. Sometimes, spouses simply have different opinions that are not easily resolved, and the surface issue may be the *only* issue. For example, Roger feels that Beth has spoiled her children. He believes that children should share in the household responsibilities, and that Beth shouldn't give them money unless they do something to earn it. But Beth believes her children have suffered enough from their parents' divorce, and she wants to let them be as carefree as possible. Beth and Roger have different ideas about how the children should be treated, but they can listen to each other's point of view, discuss their differences calmly, and reach an agreement that both can accept. That's how they know that they are discussing the real issue and not a decoy.

Conflict also occurs when partners think they disagree but in fact do not. These misunderstandings can be just as painful as quarrels in which the issues are "real," whether obvious or muddied by underlying fears. One remarried couple had a series of arguments about lovemaking. Major fights grew from exchanges like the following.

HUSBAND: Are you feeling alright?

WIFE: I could be better.

HUSBAND: Then let's just turn off the light and go to sleep.

WIFE: (Resentfully) If that's what you want.

What happened here? This man's first wife had been embarrassed by direct requests, so he had developed an indirect approach. But when his second wife heard a question about her health, she interpreted it as an attempt to avoiding lovemaking, and she felt rejected and angry. He, in turn, interpreted her response, "I could be better," as a refusal to the question he never directly asked. Instead of enabling them to enjoy the closeness they both wanted, this couple's poor communication sentenced them to fighting about whose libido was at fault.

Regardless of the conflict trigger, we react by trying to defend ourselves. We feel we must convince our partners that we are right and they are wrong, and when logic doesn't seem to work, we often resort to personal attack. And once personal accusations are brought into an argument, we will fight over these concerns before turning to the issue that promoted the disagreement.

The more aggressive the personal attack, the less its chance of success. If we yield to force, we feel bad about ourselves, our spouse, and our relationship. To prevent those feelings, we often choose to dig in our heels and resist coercion any way we can. If we do concede, we make an entry in our book of grievances. And while we often fail to repay our spouses' favors, we never forget to redress a wrong. Not only are all injuries repaid, but we give back a little more than we received, as if we're trying to compensate for having conceded.

So couples begin a vicious cycle in which each act of intimate terrorism provokes a more severe response. Soon arguments replace negotiation, and distrust shadows the couple's chance of happiness together.

Few marital breakups, as mentioned earlier, are caused by major betrayals or disasters; most result from small but frequent acts of inconsideration, disrespect, and hostility. So it's crucial to learn constructive ways of dealing with differences while they're still minor. Those of us who have seen one marriage fail because we let small things build up should do everything we can to prevent a repeat of the pattern. Fortunately, conflict does not have to be destructive. If handled well, and used sparingly, it can be a source of strength in marriage.

The Natural History of Marital Conflict

Problems tend to arise whenever two people have different and incompatible views of a given situation. Unfortunately, we all cling to our personal beliefs and behaviors. Our very essence seems to be challenged when anyone disagrees with us or criticizes our behavior. "No one who dislikes what I say or do can like or respect me" seems to be embedded in our brains. So when disagreement occurs, we generally spend more energy in self-defense and counterattack than in trying to understand and resolve the issue in an intelligent way.

One error lies in our tendency to think in terms of absolute rights and wrongs. We often feel there can be only one "right" view of things, and any alternative must be wrong. Because we all believe our position is the right one, the other must be wrong, and anyone who disagrees with us implies that our view is the one that must be wrong.

Absolute thinking dooms us to needless expenditure of energy deciding who is guilty or innocent, who started it and who simply reacted as any reasonable person would. Naturally, we all want to be innocent, so we blame the other guy. When we do admit guilt, we generally point out that our negative behavior was a reasonable response to the other person's unreasonable behavior. With both partners writing off their negatives as logical consequences of the other's actions, protests of personal innocence and partner's villainy quickly obscure the real issue.

Roger and Beth fell into the trap of holding the other person completely responsible for problems. Before marriage, they were inseparable, but after a few months of marriage, Beth wanted to resume her own social activities with friends. When Roger objected, claiming that she seemed to want to be single again, Beth said he was too possessive. She felt he was suspicious of her most innocent encounters: even when she was with women friends, Roger asked questions that led her to believe he suspected her of trying to meet men. Because she was unwilling to give up her friends, Beth started to mislead Roger about how she spent her time. It was easier, she thought, to make up stories than to deal with Roger's mistaken suspicions.

Roger, on the other hand, felt he had good reasons not to trust Beth. Once, when she had been very angry at him, she told him that she could easily support herself both emotionally and financially. Sometimes her comments led him to believe she thought she'd given up too much freedom in marrying him. Roger was also hurt any time she mentioned meeting a man she considered interesting or attractive. Since Beth had left her first husband for him, Roger imagined she was capable of leaving him if a better prospect came along.

Roger and Beth both felt victimized. Beth didn't think of herself as a liar; it was Roger's irrational jealousy that forced her to lie to keep the peace. Roger hated being suspicious, but Beth's complaints and deceptions made mistrust his only "reasonable" defense. In short, each saw the other person's negative behavior as the cause of his or her own negative response, and each felt right while the other was wrong.

For one person to be right and the other wrong, each would have to act independently. In marriage, however, all behaviors are interdependent. Each action influences every other action, and each person both initiates and reacts simultaneously. Marital interaction is a neverending circle, and any attempt to determine who was wrong initially is as arbitrary as it is hopeless.

One typical marital conflict cycle is the nagging wife and the withdrawn husband. Husbands will complain that their wives' nagging forces them to withdraw to escape. The wives of these men are equally vehement in complaining that their husbands are so uncommunicative or uncooperative that messages have to be repeated before they are heard. If you talk with only the husband or the wife, either position sounds sensible. No one wants to be nagged, and no one wants to live with a person who refuses to communicate or cooperate.

Let's look at a specific interaction between husband and wife. In this situation, the husband has just picked up his tennis racket and is heading for the front door:

SHE: I thought we were going to clean the house this morning!

HE: Stop nagging me about the housework. I'll do it later.

SHE: You've been saying "later" for over a week and you still haven't done any work.

The husband and wife would describe this short sequence very differently. She would say that he provoked her by leaving to play tennis when he had promised to help clean the house. Then, when she reminded him of his promise, he accused her of nagging and refused to change his plans. He would say that she started nagging him about housework without bothering to find out that he intended to do it after his tennis game. When he told her that he would do it later, she accused him of making promises he had no intention of keeping. Both describe or "punctuate" their accounts by sandwiching one of their own innocent responses between two of the other's hostile or provoking actions.

Changing punctuation can alter the way we view any interaction. For example, if the wife had acknowledged that she knew about the tennis game for hours but waited until he was almost out the door before reminding him about the housework, her husband would seem more like a victim of unnecessary nagging. On the other hand, if he admitted that he often postponed doing his share of housework until she gave up and did it herself, he would no longer appear so innocent.

Disagreement about how to punctuate a sequence of

events is at the root of countless marital struggles. We view most arguments in a way that supports our innocence and our partners' guilt. In our attempts at self justification, we often try to convince our partners of our innocence and reasonableness. But because being right is as important to our partners as to us, arguments quickly escalate over whose punctuation of events is closer to the truth. Since punctuation is inherently arbitrary, we end up battling over subjective viewpoints. Each person claims to have an objective standard of right and wrong, a standard that is nonexistent.

Arguments over punctuation can never end logically. Typically, the initial issue is long forgotten as both partners engage in defensive aggression. Each attacks the other in order to justify self and weaken the force of the other's attack. When this happens, the conflict shifts to secondary issues which usually defy definition, much less resolution.

The resulting spirals not only fail to resolve the conflict, but they have an insidious way of creating in our partners the behaviors that we like least. When we hold fast to our own perspectives, and refuse to see the other side, our actions only confirm our partners' accusations. We don't realize this, of course, because we fail to recognize our role in the creation of our own distress. But since every defensive reaction is experienced by our partners as an attack, our own defensiveness provokes our partners' defensiveness and further aggression. Thus, often unknowingly, we become the architects of our own unhappiness.

Roger and Beth provide a further example. Here, Beth has walked into the house at 8 P.M. on a Monday night, after a weekend of argument with her husband over whether she should deal with her ex-husband's delinquent child-support payments in person or by phone.

ROGER: Where were you?
BETH: I told you I was working!
ROGER: You're such a liar. Your ex-husband called to say he'd be late and asked if I could get the message to you.

BETH: I decided I had to meet him in person to get the money matters settled. I knew if I told you you'd start up again and we've already been fighting about this for two days. Obviously I was right. You'd have me arguing over my support check for years by phone.

ROGER: I don't believe that money is all you discuss with that deadbeat.

After this kind of exchange, Beth probably will become a more skillful liar. She has had enough of Roger's jealous accusations, and she will continue to conceal her activities from him, no matter how innocent they might be. Roger's method of expressing concern about her lying almost guarantees that she will continue to do so.

But Beth is also helping to create the behavior she claims to detest. Roger's suspicions increase every time he discovers a lie. If she were as innocent as she claimed to be, he tells himself, there would be no need for deception. Roger and Beth are clearly encouraging the very behaviors that lead both to feel so victimized.

Spirals of behavior such as this are fueled by our tendency to use personality traits to explain our mates' negative behavior, and to use our mates' provocation or some other outside force to explain our own imperfections. As discussed earlier, we offer different explanations of our own negative behavior than for that of others. *We* do rotten things because circumstances force us to, but *they* do them because of personality flaws. This kind of reasoning allows us to feel victimized by our mates. Beth says Roger is jealous and possessive, whereas she is forced to lie because he is irrational. Roger says Beth is threatening and deceitful, whereas his behavior is merely a reasonable attempt to protect himself from possible infidelity.

As long as we explain marital problems in terms of our partners' personalities, we have no responsibility to change our own behavior. We can remain victims of our partners' unfortunate personality traits. If, instead, we understand that our partners' misbehavior is a reaction to our own, we acknowledge our role in its creation and have the power to change it. Curiously, the more we feel victimized by our partners, the longer we suffer. Conversely, the faster we accept a share of the responsibility for problems, the sooner we can achieve the happiness we seek.

It's not easy to overcome the natural tendency to blame. As Dan Greenberg and Suzanne O'Malley write in their wonderful satire, *How to Avoid Love and Marriage:* "Every single phenomenon in the entire universe is somebody's fault. The only way to absolve yourself of blame is to prove that it was somebody else's fault." In order to assure that we are never to blame, most of us employ a list of dirty-fighting techniques that only make the battle longer and more painful. Here are a few:

Name-calling. We focus on what our partner *is* instead of what he or she *does.* For example, "You are careless" rather than, "You didn't record the last three checks that you wrote."

Overgeneralizing. We move from a single observation to a general statement about things that always or never happen. The husband who forgot to buy his wife's favorite cereal is advised that he is "always thoughtless" and "never considerate."

Alluding to family patterns. We explain our partners' behavior as the result of family patterns for which we are in no way responsible. For example, instead of trying to find out why his wife is depressed, a husband might react by saying, "You're just like your mother."

Gunnysacking. We bring past or unrelated issues into the argument. For example, when accused by his second wife of giving too much money to his ex-wife, a husband might say, "I don't know how you can complain when you only work part-time."

Using counter-accusations. We ignore any criticism we receive and respond instead by putting down our partner.

For example, if a husband suggested that his wife get more exercise, she might respond, "I might not be in good shape, but at least *I* don't need three martinis every night."

Mind-reading. We tell our partners what they are thinking or feeling, as though only we knew the truth. One wife complained that her husband always accused her of deliberately starting fights. Even when she denied it, he would say "You might not be aware of it, but you obviously want to get into an argument."

Approaches such as these introduce distracting irrelevancies into the discussion and provoke the other person to retaliate. These maneuvers are better adapted to confusing the issue and inflicting pain than to reaching agreement and reestablishing intimacy.

A lack of resolution is not the only negative outcome of this kind of arguing. After many personal attacks, spouses will feel deprived of the appreciation and respect they deserve, and eventually will question their relationship. As commitment weakens, there is even less reason to restrain anger, and conflicts become increasingly bitter. Eventually, hope of making things better is lost, and the survival of the marriage is threatened.

Most of us don't like to fight, and we sometimes simply withdraw in an attempt to avoid or stop an argument. In the heat of conflict, when one person tires of the fight, he or she will often say something like:

"You win. We'll do it your way."
"We never get anywhere, so let's not discuss this again."
"I can't take this anymore. I'm going out for a while."
"I don't want to talk about it."

Obviously, when conflict is interrupted, the issue cannot be resolved. That would be fine if issues, like old soldiers, faded away. But the issue lingers, builds in importance, and finds its way onto a list of sidetracking accusations in the next major conflict. Therefore, what is claimed to be a way to avoid or end the conflict is just another form of escalation.

Another way of trying to avoid conflict is to simply suppress anger and not allow overt fights to start. However, even when we avoid negative comments, our nonverbal cues clearly indicate our distress. When we are asked what the problem is, we can always say something like:

> "Oh, I don't know. I guess I'm just tired."
> "I had a bad day at work today."
> "I have a headache."
> "Nothing. (sigh)"

These reactions don't avoid conflict; at best they delay it. Shelved problems are certain to return. But when they do, the context will be different and the problem may be even harder to resolve.

One remarried husband resented having to provide most of the financial support for his wife's three children. He liked his stepchildren, but he felt their father should be contributing much more. Whenever his wife suspected that he was unhappy and asked him what was bothering him, he offered excuses that had nothing to do with the real problem. Not wanting to upset his wife, he kept his feelings to himself, or so he thought. Actually, he managed to express his feelings in other ways. Whenever the children asked for extra money, he would deny their requests, and complain about their greed or ungratefulness. He also became extremely critical of the children, in part to justify his unwillingness to give them more money. His wife was much more distressed by these harsh judgments of her children than she would have been by an open discussion of money matters.

Although it's usually best to deal with issues when they arise, there are times when it is wiser *not* to do so. These are the occasions when one person is particularly tense, moody, or hypersensitive for other reasons. Sometimes we actually do have bad days at the office, headaches, premenstrual ten-sion, or fatigue. Our distress may have nothing to do with our spouses, but given the slightest provocation, we will dump our pent-up emotion in our partners' unsuspecting (and undeserving) laps.

Many people believe they have no control over their outbursts, but this is far from the truth. Many of us have high stress jobs where we may feel provoked by our boss and coworkers a dozen times a day. At work, we learn to suppress irritation and anger. At home, however, the smallest irritations can seem unbearable. But it's just as important to control ourselves at home as at work. We can start to assume control by trying to avoid conflict under circumstances in which we are most likely to handle it poorly.

When you know that even the smallest conflict is likely to trigger a major confrontation, it's a good idea to explain your feelings to your partner and ask if it would be alright to talk about the issue later. Delaying conflict in this way can be helpful if two conditions are met: first, recognize that an issue has arisen and offer to resolve it at a specific and not too distant later time; then ask if your partner is comfortable with temporarily delaying the discussion. This approach, when reserved for the times when it is really needed, and not used as a means of attempting to escape discussion, can prevent unnecessary stress.

Resolving Conflict

While avoidance and suppression don't work in resolving conflict, other approaches do. Peaceful, effective resolution involves a special effort, since self-defense in conflict situations is such a natural response. Fortunately, there are ways to minimize the bitterness of conflict and arrive more quickly at a mutually satisfying resolution.

Before getting into technique, it's important to agree about some fundamental beliefs that enhance our ability to turn a fight into a problem-solving discussion. First, we should accept the fact that differences of opinion, though not generally enjoyable, are not catastrophic. Rather, they are an inevitable outcome of our decision to share our lives with another human being. When handled well, a discussion of differences can actually be helpful. We learn more about each other, which can bring us closer together, and we learn about other ways of looking at life, which helps us develop as individuals. It's important to believe that no matter what differences arise, a cooperative exploration of alternatives will almost certainly lead to an acceptable resolution.

In almost any marital conflict, both partners can win. In a destructive conflict pattern, of course, each person tries to win at the other's expense. The loser will eventually get revenge, and in time the relationship must suffer as spouses take turns defeating each other. In contrast, the "two-winner" model is based on cooperation rather than competition. Both partners consider themselves equally worthwhile, each has a view that deserves serious consideration, and each is interested in preserving the relationship. When these assumptions are shared, partners start working with, instead of against, each other.

When cooperation becomes more important than competition, we can set aside our attacking/defensive stances and relax enough to focus on the issue. But figuring out exactly what the issue is can be difficult, because partners will define the problem differently. And unfortunately, both definitions usually include some negative assumptions about the other that contain seeds of conflict. Regrettably, we almost never check out these assumptions.

For example, Steve realizes that Rosa deeply loved her first husband, Ron. After Ron died in an auto accident, Rosa fell into deep mourning. She met Steve about a year later and married him within months. It was Steve who pressed for an early wedding date, and it is Steve who now has some doubts about whether Rosa has really given up her love for Ron.

Every time Rosa complains about their old station wagon and suggests that they buy a new car, and every time she suggests a winter vacation, Steve fears the worst. Because

Ron liked sports cars and skiing, Steve is afraid that Rosa is trying to reincarnate him as Ron. Steve now refuses to buy a new car or take trips anywhere near snow. Unfortunately, Steve is self-conscious about his fear and never discusses it; Rosa, in turn, feels that he simply ignores her requests out of self-interest.

Each spouse has a pat explanation for the other's behavior. Both explanations are inaccurate, and both spouses suffer because of their false interpretations. If they took the time to find out whether their worst fears were correct, each would discover that the other held the most positive possible view: each earnestly wants the other's love and respect. To avoid allowing inaccurate interpretations of your partner's motives to create problems where none exist, it's very important to follow this principle:

When you feel angry with your spouse, assume that the problem lies in your inability to understand the issue from your partner's point of view. Before reacting to what you think is the problem, learn everything you can about your partner's view of the situation.

Many conflicts can be averted simply by asking instead of assuming. All too often, we add up the facts and assume the worst, but from another point of view, those same facts can have a completely different meaning. For example, if Roger asks Beth how she spent the day, Beth could interpret that as checking up on her, but Roger may have simply been trying to start a conversation. Or if Roger sees Beth looking intently at another man, he may assume she is interested in the man, whereas she might be wondering where she can buy Roger a shirt like the one the man is wearing. Once we learn another way to look at the facts, fights often become unnecessary.

After gaining a clear understanding of your partner's view, it's time to state your own. As in all good communication, the challenge here is to state your views openly, but tactfully. Here are a few suggestions:

1. *Use descriptions rather than judgments.* This keeps your partner's defensiveness to a minimum by putting the focus on behavior rather than personality. For example, if a wife doesn't like the way her husband treats their children, she might say, "I think you could have paid more attention to the kids," but not "You don't care about the kids," or "You're so distant and uncommunicative."

2. *Use specific rather than general language.* Statements like "You're always late," or "You never do things the way I like them done," evoke more hostility and defensiveness than change. On the other hand, statements like "I'd like you to call me if you are going to be late," or "It's easier for me if you put the tools in the workroom," are reasonable and specific enough to make the point.

3. *Express your concerns in a timely fashion.* Since there's no use arguing about things that can't be changed, comments should be oriented toward the future rather than the past. For example, "I'd like to go bowling next Friday night" is far more useful than "I wish we'd gone bowling. That movie was awful." Requests for the future can be granted, while criticisms of the past leave both of you frustrated.

Once you and your partner can listen and express yourselves with directness moderated by tact, you are ready to define the problem. In many cases, even when partners understand each other's point of view, they will still feel their own view makes more sense. But in the improved emotional climate, both should be more open to suggestions. Once again, the best way to avoid escalation is to keep disagreement from deteriorating into a personal attack. It's crucial not to hear "You are bad," when the message should be "What you believe is different from what I believe."

When you both define the problem in the same terms, you and your partner can then discuss possible solutions. If you can't agree about the issue, find a resolution that embraces both points of view. Cooperation is the key here. In searching for solutions, each partner should have the chance to make

suggestions that will take both points of view into consideration.

Next, you must arrive at consensus. You do not have to
define the situation in the same way, but the solution must
be acceptable to both. For example, if she wants her children
to accompany them on all vacations, and he wants to spend
vacations alone with his new wife, they may agree that the
children will accompany them on some but not all trips.

Finally, it's important to find ways to avoid future conflict.
When the fight has ended and both partners feel calm again,
it's tempting to simply forget the matter and hope it never
happens again. Unfortunately, most couples continue to
quarrel about the same things. To break this pattern, *no
conflict should come to an end until the couple has agreed
upon a mutually acceptable way to prevent its recurrence.*

Fran and Ed often fight when he comes home late without
calling. The specifics of their plan to prevent future fights
depend upon the basic issue of the arguments. If Fran is
annoyed because the dinners she prepares get cold or burnt
when Ed comes home late, they may decide that she will only
cook if he can assure her that he will be home on time. If her
concern is that he doesn't care enough to let her know when
he will be late, they may decide that he will call every time
he'll be more than half an hour late.

It's also possible that Ed might feel Fran doesn't care
enough to offer sympathy when he has a hard day at work.
If so, they can decide that she will ask him about his day no
matter what time he comes in. An effective plan for preven-
tion *must* consider the underlying issues of the argument.

The best plans for avoiding future arguments are ones in
which each partner takes some responsibility for acting differently when the trigger situation arises. That way, each
person has some control, and neither is asked to accept all
the blame. You may want to put your agreements in writing
so you will be more likely to remember them and less likely
to fight about the details later. A form for this purpose is
provided at the end of the chapter.

Let's review once again the ways to make conflict constructive:

1.   Agree that conflict is not a catastrophe, and that you both still respect each other and the relationship. Agree to use the two-winner model.
2.   Exchange points of view, making sure you both ask questions and check out your understanding. Explain points of view openly, but tactfully. Don't fight dirty.
3.   Define the problem, acknowledging both points of view. Focus on issues, not personalities.
4.   Search for solutions.
5.   Arrive at an agreement that is acceptable to both.
6.   Make some plans or resolutions for how to avoid similar conflicts in the future.

Reading and understanding these guidelines is only the first step toward making them work. It takes commitment, patience, and a lot of practice to resolve differences fairly and tactfully. The benefits, however, are worth the effort. You and your spouse will feel more understood, accepted, and respected by each other, and as these feelings increase, conflict is likely to diminish.

Containing Conflict

We can't eliminate all conflict from our lives. Sometimes we are so irritated, hurt, or angry that we're unwilling to try to understand our partner's point of view. We aren't interested in constructive change, but only in protecting and defending ourselves. Other times, we simply want to get our way, without having to explain or negotiate.

Anticipating these times of disharmony, we need to learn how to contain conflict when it occurs, preventing it from getting too serious or too frequent. In learning how to contain conflict, we have to begin with an understanding of how marital conflict develops.

There are six stages to every fight.

1. Conflicts begin when A pulls the *trigger* that provokes B. The triggers can be words or actions, and they can be intentional or not.

2. B responds to the provocation in a *defensive* way, by self-justifying, protectively withdrawing, or by verbal or physical attack.

3. A reacts to B's anger by *escalating* in equally defensive ways.

4. After a time, the intensity of their anger subsides a bit and they enter the *commitment stage* of conflict. Each feels insulted or rejected, and each is determined to retaliate or protect against further hurt. This is the time for sulking and sarcastic remarks.

5. Eventually, A or B will decide that being angry or withdrawn is more painful than trying to resolve the conflict. That person will attempt a *reconciliation*.

6. *Resolution* of the issue may be temporary or permanent depending on the care and thoughtfulness put into the agreement.

At each of these points, both partners can make important choices that will influence the frequency and intensity of their disagreements.

When a conflict is triggered, we can choose which battles to wage rather than argue about every minor issue that arises. In a typical day, we can find fault with a vast number of small details. Couples have been known to go to war over burning the toast, parking the car two inches over the midline of the garage, or forgetting to wash a glass. Petty concerns are inevitable when two individuals live in the same house and share their lives. If we rise to every opportunity to start a fight, we would have time for nothing but conflict. Therefore, whenever we are irritated, we should decide whether or not to mention it.

Constant criticism over small details gives rise to a climate of rejection which leads to withdrawal and/or counterattack. Also, it's harder to gain serious consideration of important criticism when it is lost in a sea of petty complaints.

While it's important to choose which issues to raise, it's equally important to guard against defensive responses. Sometimes the wife who thinks her husband spends too much time with children from his first marriage lets it pass when he makes plans to see them. At other times, she says she would like him to spend more time with her or to include her in his activities with the children. Her husband has a choice when the issue is raised. He can hear it as a criticism of his lack of love for her and an intrusion upon his parental responsibilities, or he can hear it as an expression of her desire to be with him. It is always safest to make a positive interpretation until proven wrong. That way, you'll never be guilty of having fights over issues that never existed.

When you do make a negative interpretation, remember to check it out before you react. Couples who follow this rule can avoid 99 of every 100 domestic squabbles.

We can also control conflicts by learning what triggers our anger. We all have sore spots—areas in which we are especially sensitive to criticism. These issues attach like magnets to unrelated issues. We can help each other by identifying the triggers that are sure to set us off. Some may be trivial, others important, but all are guaranteed to elicit hurt or anger. Once we acknowledge our own sore spots, we can identify our overreactions and control our decisions about expressing anger. Awareness of the sensitive areas of others allows us to avoid saying or doing the things most likely to provoke confrontation.

A husband may be mildly irritated when his wife says he drives too fast, or eats too much. It bothers him more when she complains that he doesn't keep his promises about helping around the house and when she talks while he is watching TV. And it sends him into an absolute rage when she says he is stupid or compares him unfavorably to her ex-husband.

Awareness of his reaction patterns can allow this husband

more control over his responses. He might decide to save his anger for the major irritations, and he could find ways to react more constructively to some of the recurring triggers. His wife's knowledge of what triggers his anger allows her to have more control of the reactions she elicits. She may decide to avoid provoking an argument, or if she feels severely attacked herself, she may pull out all the stops. Armed with this knowledge, both spouses are much less likely to unintentionally start and escalate conflicts.

In order to become aware of the sensitive areas in your own relationship, you and your partner can use the space below to list the things that cause mild, moderate, or major irritation:

	Husband	Wife
Mild irritations		
Moderate irritations		
Major sensitivities		

There are times, of course, when an argument will escalate to the point where both partners are committed to staying angry. Since unresolved conflict almost always lapses into sulky withdrawal, it's important to find ways to keep the sulking from going on too long.

In the commitment stage of anger, we make the no-win decision to punish ourselves and our partners. Each spouse develops more and more hostile feelings about the other without gaining perspective on their subjective angry interpretations of the issue. When we are sulking and withdrawing from our partners, we ultimately have only three choices. We can spend the rest of our lives sulking, we can get a divorce, or we can reach out and make amends. Since we usually intend to make up eventually, we can minimize the damage to the relationship by ending the withdrawal as soon as possible. No issue can be resolved until caring communication is resumed.

How do we decide when to end the withdrawal? One way is to wait for our partners to make the first move. We are often tempted to hold out until others apologize, so as not to risk any more hurt. But since both spouses are feeling vulnerable, and neither is anxious to make the first move, the withdrawal can be unnecessarily prolonged.

As an alternative, we can take the responsibility for initiating contact as soon as possible. Often, we're not motivated to reach out until the pain of separation is greater than the pain of arguing, and two people seldom reach this point at the same time. But if both partners try to hasten their own willingness to reestablish closeness, the periods of separation won't last as long.

Someone has to gently invite the resumption of friendly communication. For example, after one husband had barricaded himself in his garage workshop for two hours following a minor skirmish, his wife went to him and simply said "I miss you. Can't we be friends again?" She makes no admission of guilt; all she does is reaffirm her commitment to him. He can accept or reject the invitation. He is likely to accept if the invitation is conveyed with caring and respect. He is unlikely to give in to a demand such as "This has gone on long enough. Are you ready to stop being such a jerk?"

Of course, the husband can also invite a reconciliation by taking the first step to end the withdrawal that he initiated. As soon as either partner is able to risk reaching out to the other, that person should take the chance. When both partners assume responsibility for reestablishing contact, the fight can be brought to a quicker and more honorable end.

Instead of just apologizing or asking to make up, we usually give little signs that indicate our willingness to end the argument. One woman clams up and won't speak when she has decided to stay angry; starting a conversation is her way of indicating that she is ready to make up. Her husband withdraws physically; he can indicate his readiness for closeness by reaching out and touching his wife. Spouses can teach each other the personal signals they will use to end a disagreement. You and your partner may want to list the ways in which you would like to signal a willingness to make up.

SIGNALS FOR MAKING UP

	Husband	*Wife*
How you would like to make up		
How you would like your partner to make up		

Conflict generally ends with a resolution. Sometimes the resolution is no more than an agreement to stop fighting. But when this is all that happens, the issues generally resurface as though they had never been discussed before. In order to achieve a more permanent resolution, every marital argument should end with a new rule designed to prevent repetitions of the same issue in the future.

Keeping a conflict resolution log can be helpful. Among other things, the log identifies the focal issue of each argument. This identification may not be as easy as it seems because two people who are arguing usually have very different interpretations of what's going on. Therefore, it's best to characterize the issue according to the actions that served as a trigger—not the meaning assigned to them. For example, "Marge talked on the phone for three hours straight" or "Bill left the tank on empty after using the car." If you use interpretations rather than the events themselves, your list will be redundant because, as you now know, most of our fights center on only one issue—whether or not our partners love and respect us as we think they should.

In the center column of the conflict resolution log, list any unfair fight techniques either partner uses, in order to help each person become aware of tendencies to resort to tactics like mindreading, name calling, or counteraccusations. It's better to start by identifying your own tactics before pointing out the mistakes of the other, since this exercise is designed to prevent rather than encourage conflict. Once you are aware of your tendency to resort to coercive techniques, it will be easier to start working on controlling their use.

In the final column, write down mutually-satisfactory rules with which you and your partner conclude your disagreement. As mentioned earlier, except in rare situations when both agree that one was at fault, these rules should involve changes by both spouses. For example, one wife was angry at her husband for allowing her stepchildren to refuse to eat their salads and still get dessert. She felt he was undermining her authority since she prepared the meals and felt that the kid's eating habits were her responsibility. Her husband was equally angry at her for criticizing him in front of the children.

Since each felt the other did something very wrong, their resolution should involve changes from each of them. The husband's change could be agreeing to leave to his wife the decisions about what the children should or shouldn't eat, or he might agree that he won't change her rules without discussing them with her. The wife might agree that she will raise her objections in private rather than in front of the kids. The exact details of their agreement are less important than the fact that they agree on the new rules, and that neither feels exploited.

You might reread the list of rules from time to time to remind yourselves of the agreements. Adhering to these rules should help avoid recurrence of arguments over the same issue. Of course, the rules may have to be revised from time to time. Situations will change, and rules that were effective at the end of one conflict may breed disagreement later. When it seems as though a rule is not working well, it's wise to take a few minutes to discuss and revise it when you both are relaxed.

A Final Note

Because we all occasionally hurt and offend each other, due to lack of knowledge, skill, or caring, there is one final element of conflict resolution necessary in any intimate relationship: forgiveness. We need to use a generous amount of forgiveness in order to repair inevitable hurts and continue to grow together as a couple. When all is said and done, *forgiveness is one of the strongest expressions of love.*

CONFLICT LOG

Date	Issue	Dirty Tactics	New Rules

8
Balancing Home and Work

*E*very man and woman could use a good wife. What a luxury to have a partner who eagerly and competently performs all the mundane and tedious tasks necessary to keep home and family functioning. Of course, our wives would not just be housekeepers. They would be intelligent, interesting, dynamic, self-confident helpmates who devote themselves to making our lives easy and pleasant, and who are happy to put our needs and desires before their own.

Sadly, perfect wives are as hard to find as the equally intelligent and interesting perfect husbands who earn a lot of money without working much, put their families before all else, and reliably and sensitively strive to do everything possible to please their mates. Most of us are likely to find the answer to our dreams only by inventing an imaginary friend.

Many of us suffered disappointments in our first marriages when our mates didn't meet our expectations about the handling of work and home responsibilities. We may feel our first spouse worked too much or not enough. We may recall that we did more than our share of housework for less than our share of appreciation. Or we may feel our first spouse hindered rather than helped our career aspirations.

We usually blame our ex-spouses for our conflicts and disappointments, and we expect spouse number two to be more cooperative. For example, a workaholic man whose first wife felt neglected may simply expect his second wife to be more understanding. A woman whose first husband did nothing around the house may insist that her second husband take at least 50 percent of all household responsibility. Non-negotiable expectations can lead to disaster in a second marriage. Only when we are willing to settle for something less than perfect can we start discussing compromises that will please both husband and wife.

Women and men often bring different expectations about work to their second marriages. Women who remarry have different work histories than those marrying for the first time. Some have always expected to work regardless of marriage or children. Others interrupted careers when they had children, and returned to work when their marriages ended. Still others never worked outside the home while married, and entered the work force, often for the first time, when their first marriage ended.

Whatever their work situation when married, women who divorce suffer a drop in their standard of living by around 40 percent. Left with a pressing need for money, most divorced women find themselves working out of necessity if not by choice.

Work experience after divorce has the most profound impact on divorcees from traditional marriages. They are forced to trade the role of homemaker for that of working woman, or far more often, working mother. This change may be painful initially, but once women realize they can support themselves financially, they are reluctant to become dependent again. After a marriage has ended, it's hard to ignore the possibility that a second marriage might also fail. Therefore, whether they have always valued work or whether they learned from experience, most remarrying women want to preserve a degree of economic independence.

Nevertheless, there is a group of women who would like to work less or not at all. Some women in their 30s feel the pressure of the biological time clock, and want to start a family or continue to build one. They may be eager to set their jobs aside or reduce the number of hours they work in order to devote more time to children.

When a second marriage involves combining families, women who were happily involved in a career may feel obligated to spend more time at home helping the children adjust to the new situation. And if more children are born, these women face the dilemma common to many modern mothers. They are reluctant to stay out of the work force too long, but also feel reluctant to spend too much time away from their children.

Unfortunately, many second marriages include financial obligations that make it difficult, if not impossible, for the wife to be unemployed. Husbands who are supporting children from a previous marriage may be unwilling or unable to support two families singlehandedly. And stepfathers without children of their own may be reluctant to work to provide for stepchildren who are not receiving support from their fathers.

It is clear that a wife's decision about whether to work and how much to work is often complex and influenced by many factors. In contrast, few men feel they have the freedom to decide whether or not to work. Society's increased acceptance of working women has not diminished the expectation that men be the breadwinners. In fact, most men create and maintain a large part of their identities through their work.

The clash between traditional and modern values accounts for a diversity of views held by men about working wives. Some men, especially younger ones, do not expect to be the sole source of support for their families, but many others are ambivalent or even disapproving of working wives. Some were formerly married to women who gave up their jobs for motherhood, and they grew accustomed to having their clothes taken to the cleaners, their kids driven to after-school activities, and their houses kept clean by their wives. Whether the arrangement was due to traditional role expectations or a negotiated expression of preferences, these men may prefer the traditional model of marriage. Other men believe their ex-wives' work contributed in some way to the breakup of the marriage, and are wary about a repeat experience. In their view, the stability of their second marriages rests on their wives' staying at home.

When husbands and wives have different opinions about wives' work, conflict is inevitable. When arguments about whether the wife should work are complicated by disagreements about who is to take care of the home, the marriage may cave in under the strain. Therefore every remarrying couple needs to reach agreement about the distribution of work and home responsibilities. There are no absolutes, so every couple must find its own solution. After putting the major challenges in perspective, we will offer guidelines for achieving a satisfying agreement.

The Predominance of Traditional Roles

According to the Bureau of Labor Statistics, the number of women in the work force is steadily rising, and today 67 percent of all married women work at least part-time. Given the fact that 95 percent of all husbands also work, 62 percent of today's couples have two wage-earners. About two-thirds of wives who work hold full-time jobs, including more than half of the mothers of children of all ages. Their earnings make a substantial contribution to family income.

Unfortunately, our values and behavior have not kept pace with the changing roles of women. One might expect that as women share more of the traditional male responsibilities, men would reciprocate by taking on a greater share of the traditional female duties. But studies of two-earner couples have revealed, probably to the surprise of few women, that traditional roles are resistant to change, and women who work outside the home still bear almost all the responsibility for domestic chores. In fact, even men who profess egalitarian social ideals are unlikely to demonstrate them by sharing the housework equally, and even unemployed husbands generally do less housework than wives who have full-time outside jobs. It's no wonder, then, that most discussions of the work/home balance are aimed at women, since they are the ones expected to accommodate.

It's easy to blame men for this sorry situation, but in fact both sexes often promote traditional role beliefs. Before we can successfully make changes, we must understand the ways in which both husbands and wives put up barriers to successful role-sharing.

More men than women still accept the basic idea that the man is the provider and the woman is the homemaker. From childhood, males are trained to develop competitiveness and leadership ability so they can grow up to be good providers. Once they reach adulthood, most of their self-esteem comes from their ability to earn a good living.

When men try to cross over into "women's territory," they find barriers that seldom confront women who assume male roles. Women can wear pants, but few men can get away with wearing skirts; women can engage in typically "male" activities like fishing or baseball, but men tend to be scorned if they take on traditional female activities like knitting or sewing. It's not surprising, then, that most men are content to stay in the roles for which they've been trained and for which they are rewarded.

Women are much more likely than men to combine the roles of wage-earner and homemaker. Most college women expect to combine careers with family, yet a surprising number still accept the idea that the woman's primary place is in the home. Even among those who believe women should have dual roles, most accept a traditional division of responsibilities (i.e., he keeps up the yard and does minor repairs, while she cleans the house and takes charge of the kitchen and the kids). Moreover, many women say they derive greater satisfaction from the wife role than the worker role.

It's doubtful that the pleasures of housework are responsible for the rewards perceived in the wife role. The satisfaction is more likely to come from being the major source of emotional support to all family members. Observation reveals that in most families, traditional role expectations prevail regardless of competence. For example, even if the husband has a degree in developmental psychology, the wife is likely to provide therapeutic and child management services for the family, and to provide the emotional support her husband desires. The rewards of this role may be intangible, but they are often emotionally fulfilling.

We can understand why working women are happy to assume responsibility for nurturing their husbands and children, but why do they also do most of the housework? Some 40 percent of earner wives have *sole* responsibility for cleaning house and caring for the children, while about two thirds have *sole* responsibility for grocery shopping and washing clothes.

One explanation for this imbalance in workloads is the fact that many women also accept traditional role distinctions. Most working wives earn less than their husbands, and the typical wife assumes that as long as her husband earns more, he has little or no obligation at home. Even when earnings are equal, if wives work by choice rather than from financial necessity, they believe they work for their own enjoyment, and therefore feel they don't have a right to expect their husbands to relieve them of any of the traditional female duties.

Even when women feel overloaded by this arrangement, they may be reluctant to give up their territory. Perhaps because of their upbringing, many women feel they have higher standards than their husbands do, and they can't trust their husbands to carry out household chores adequately. According to many husbands' standards, the kitchen floor (if they are responsible for it) is clean if your feet don't stick to it when you walk. But many wives have been programmed to feel guilty if the floor is not sparkling clean. While the husband may be doing what he considers to be a reasonably good job, his wife may be seething as she waits for him to start. As a result, many wives decide it isn't worth the trouble it takes to induce their husbands to do an adequate job, so they just do the work themselves. Cynics might wonder whether some men deliberately cultivate incompetence to avoid boring, thankless household tasks.

If you're happy with the way you now divide work and home responsibilities, there's no need to change. But if either or both of you are unhappy, you should try to work out a new arrangement. We'll help you choose by describing the four basic models commonly used to balance work and home duties.

Four Models of Balancing Family and Work

Only two of four family/work patterns have received much attention in the literature. One option is the traditional marriage in which only the husband works outside the home. The other is the two-career couple in which both spouses are committed to their jobs.

For many of us, neither option provides the satisfaction we desire. Fortunately, there are two other models from which to choose. We can have a career/earner marriage in which one partner has a stronger commitment to a profession than the other. We can also have a two-earner marriage in which both partners work primarily to earn money, and neither is committed to career above all else.

Both of these choices are based on the distinction between a career and a job. We view a career as the pursuit of work as an end in itself. Satisfaction with the job is as important as the money earned. Because the work offers intrinsic rewards, careerists often choose to devote more of their time and energy to their jobs than to their family and friends. A job, on the other hand, is essentially either a way of earning money or of just getting out of the house. A job does provide a chance to build self-esteem or to get stimulation that can't be found at home, but the job itself is less rewarding than time spent with family and friends. We can devote the same number of hours daily to a career and a job, but people close to us always know whether they are of primary or secondary importance in our lives. So the career/job distinction is as much a matter of attitude as of time.

The distribution of power and responsibility varies predictably according to the model you use. No model is necessarily better than the others, and you must choose the one that best suits your needs as a couple.

The Traditional Model. Even though a majority of wives work, as many as 34 percent of husbands and 25 percent of wives believe they should not. When only the husband works outside the home, the couple may have less money, but they do have more time for shared activities that increase enjoyment of their relationship. Conflicts over housework are also less likely to occur because the wife generally considers housekeeping as part of her job.

When there are children, the mother (or stepmother) can give the children more of her attention and energy. Although there are no conclusive findings as to the effect of mothers' employment on their children, many women still feel some guilt about working, at least when their children are young.

Women who do not work are not necessarily better mothers, but they almost certainly feel less guilty about the role they have chosen. It has also been found that when wives stay at home, couples fight less about how the children are being raised. When the mother spends all day with the children, the father usually considers their management to be primarily her responsibility, and he is likely to defer to her decisions.

Finally, whether or not a wife works outside the home, she often assumes most of the responsibility for attending to the marital relationship. In a sense, this is part of the "job" of traditional wives. The wisdom of this arrangement is debatable, but a wife who doesn't work outside the home certainly will have more time and energy to put into the relationship.

It is now almost a cliché to point out the disadvantages of the traditional model, but since many couples still choose it, they should be aware of the costs. Perhaps the greatest liability is the imbalance of power that exists when only one partner works. Since money is essentially equated with power in our society, husbands in traditional marriages have most of the power. As already mentioned, both men and women often accept the equation of money with power, though women are growing increasingly dissatisfied with the arrangement and many point out that the economic value of housework is not insignificant. In one national survey, even men estimated that they would have to pay someone $12,700 to perform the work their wives did in maintaining their homes. Considering that these are after-tax dollars, the economic value of housework is substantial.

Even today, many traditional couples believe that the husband is the only one contributing financially, so he is accorded complete financial control. Many women still have to ask their husbands for the money that both believe is rightfully his, a process that hardly contributes to a feeling of equal partnership. In addition, women who are unhappy with their marriages often feel forced to stay with their husbands simply because of their financial dependence. Neither husband nor wife benefits from being in that bind.

Because a woman's work in the home is seldom appreciated and *never* finished, housewives often suffer low self-esteem. This is reinforced by a society that tends to regard those who do not earn money as failures. When there is no recognition for the hours spent working, and when observable accomplishments are few and short-lived, it's hard for a woman to feel proud of how she spends her time. And women who feel they should be finding fulfillment in their work at home often start to feel inadequate.

In addition, home can be an isolating and confining place. Extended time alone or only in the company of children is often boring and frustrating. Motherhood can leave women with increased responsibility but less self-confidence. In principle, work outside the home can balance these effects and make motherhood more rewarding.

Nor are women the only ones to suffer. When women are isolated and unfulfilled during the day, they often depend on their husbands for emotional and intellectual fulfillment in the evening. Many men are either unable or unwilling to provide the stimulation and appreciation their wives need. This inevitably adds stress to the relationship. In addition, men who are the sole breadwinners often feel pressured to earn as much money as possible, and may feel obligated to stay in unstimulating or stressful jobs solely for financial reasons.

When both partners are dissatisfied with the traditional arrangement, each expects the other to compensate for their sacrifices. Men caught in unpleasant work situations may be eager to stay home and relax for the evening, expecting their stay-at-home wives to nurture and adore them. But the wives, equally in need of appreciation and nurturing, are likely to want the stimulation of some outside activity. Obviously, such incompatible needs and desires do not lead to a harmonious relationship.

The Dual-Career Model. In the dual-career model, both husband and wife are committed to professional growth and development. They may place tremendous value on the relationship, but they consider their professions of equal importance.

Partners are more likely to have equal power in this relationship. Working wives have greater voice in financial decisions, simply because their financial contributions are obvious. Working wives also receive more respect from their husbands because their achievements are more easily recognized and appreciated. While most husbands minimize the importance of housework, they understand and respect the

skills necessary for a career. The two-career couple also enjoys two paychecks. In a second marriage, the extra money
may lighten the financial burden considerably.

But the situation is not without its disadvantages. In some
dual career relationships, a turning point in either partner's
career can trigger a marital crisis. Two careers never develop
in exactly the same way, and partners' career demands will
often be in conflict.

Perhaps the most common area of conflict is the decision
about where to live. Two people are seldom offered the best
possible job in the same city, and mutually satisfying decisions are hard to come by. Couples are often faced with the
prospect of one spouse making career sacrifices to accomo-
date the other, or living in different cities while each pursues
the best possible career opportunity. The growing number of
"commuter couples" attests to the increasing popularity of
both spouses putting career first, at least for a time. The
phenomenon is still too recent to have yielded divorce statistics, but even when the arrangement works, it seems to be
viable for only a very short time. And the alternative of
having one spouse make sacrifices for the other is likely to
work only if partners take turns on a basis that both consider
equitable.

Another major risk in a dual-career marriage is neglect of
the relationship. In their book the *Two-Career Couple,* Francine and Douglas Hall point out that a dual-career relationship is made up of five elements: two careers, two independent people, and one relationship. Unfortunately, the
relationship tends to get pushed aside by the other demands,
and many marriages have suffered as a result. It takes a
deliberate effort to work as hard on the relationship as on the
careers to make a two-career marriage successful.

When the need to take care of children is added to the
demands of two careers, irreconcilable conflict may result.
The basic issue for two-career couples is whether their work
will be sacrificed for family or family will be sacrificed for
work. A traditional family life and two mobile careers cannot

co-exist, and every dual-career couple must carefully examine priorities and be wary of taking on more than they can handle.

Midpoints: Two Variations. Between the extremes of the dual-career and traditional models are two dual-earner models. In the career/earner model, only one partner, usually the husband, has a career that demands a major commitment of time and energy. The other, usually the wife, works outside the home, but puts an equal or higher priority on home, children, and the marriage.

Some couples deliberately choose this model because they feel that at least one partner must devote a reasonable effort to family concerns. Others gradually drift into it, often as a result of the wife deciding to devote less time to her job after she has children.

This model works well for many couples because it retains many of the traditional divisions of responsibilities. The husband is still the primary wage-earner and the wife takes most of the home and family responsibilities. But the wife gains power and self-esteem that come from having a job.

Perhaps the major disadvantage of this model is that the wife takes on an outside job without being relieved of domestic duties. The potential for overload is tremendous, as is the potential for resentment at the apparent imbalance in responsibilities. If the woman works part-time or if the couple can afford household help, the arrangement is more likely to be successful. But when she has full-time jobs in and out of the house, the sheer volume of work can be overwhelming. And if the outside job is boring, stressful, or draining, dissatisfaction increases. Particularly when there are children, mothers may find themselves sacrificing quality time with their children to far less rewarding tasks inside and outside the home.

The second dual-earner model is one in which partners are more or less equally committed to family as well as work. In these marriages, husbands express commitment to egalatarian relationships in which neither partner is bound by traditional roles. Although wives may bear most of the domestic responsibility even in these relationships, the couple often finds compensatory ways to establish equality. Partners are more likely to distribute responsibility according to competence and preference, and both may feel freedom from the confinement of traditional roles. This leads to greater flexibility, with neither partner having to make all the career sacrifices or becoming overburdened with family responsibilities. The variety makes it more likely that each will derive more pleasure from both work and family. Perhaps the greatest beneficiaries are the children who have the opportunity to develop close relationships with both parents.

Even this model, however, has its disadvantages. Some people intellectually embrace an egalitarian model, but emotionally question their deviation from tradition. A husband may suffer some self-doubt if he doesn't achieve all he could if he devoted himself to work, and a wife may feel guilty about handing over any of her traditional responsibilities. Also, it's possible that neither partner will be able to achieve their desired level of job satisfaction or family satisfaction because of their failure to make a total commitment to either endeavor.

Clearly, each model has benefits and costs, and "having it all" may be an unrealizable dream. The best model for any couple can only be determined by a mutual evaluation of each person's interests, skills, and values. Even then, adjustments must be made for changes in family and individual needs.

No matter which model is used, as long as either spouse has a job, there is some risk that one partner may become excessively devoted to working outside the home. This is least likely to occur in the two-earner model, but it sometimes happens despite the best intentions. In the two-career models, devotion to work is part of the agreement, but couples are not always aware of the possible consequences. Any couple concerned with achieving a balance between work and home commitments must consider the problem of workaholism.

Workaholics

Even though most wives do work outside their homes, many men and women alike worry that the family will suffer as a result. On the other hand, the equally serious problem of husbands who work too much is often accepted as a virtue rather than a vice. When husbands spend too much time on the job, their wives and children pay a heavy price. Marriages are more likely to end because of conflicts about the wife's work, but the quality of the marriage can suffer tremendously when husbands become too involved in their careers.

The modern American man usually sets career goals for himself and continually strives to live up to the high standards he sets. These standards play a central role in the way men assess their achievements in life. As one research team concluded, a man will only feel good about his achievements if he can ". . . enter a career and start a family early in adulthood, be upwardly mobile, and successfully . . . provide for his family throughout his adult life."

Of course, working women also set criteria for evaluating their job performance. But their overall satisfaction is usually more determined by marital than occupational success. If their marriages succeed, women are likely to be content even if they do not attain the higher levels of professional success. Among men, however, success on the job is much more important than marital satisfaction in creating a sense of contentment with life.

Of course all men are not alike in drive for occupational success or in the extent to which career advancement offers greater satisfaction than marital success. But society reinforces a man's dedication to work, and men who are more successful are held in higher esteem by nearly everyone, including their wives.

When work is a means to an end, it's not a problem; but it is a problem when work is used to avoid other stresses or when it becomes an end in itself. As we have observed, cultural forces can prompt both men and women to over-achievement: men to demonstrate their masculinity and women to demonstrate their equality with men. But psychological factors can also explain a drive to work too much. For example, some people feel so discounted by their spouses that they invest all of their energy in gaining recognition through their work or the wealth they can attain. Others feel so stressed at home that they seek even high-pressured work situations for relief. And still others are so uneasy in intimate situations that they work long hours to avoid having to cope with their spouse's reasonable desire for closeness.

It is important to be able to tell when work reaches the status of a pathological concern. Some of the telltale warning signs occur when:

1.   Self-imposed standards call for more productivity than the job itself requires.

2.   Workers spend much of their free time thinking about solutions to work problems or worrying about obstacles to vocational success.

3.   Conflicts between the demands of work and the requests of family members are usually resolved in favor of work.

4.   Little besides work is strong enough to hold the worker's interest.

5.   Energy goes into finding excuses *to work* rather than into finding reasons *not to work*.

6.   The number of hours spent at work significantly exceeds formal requirements.

It's not clear that the pursuit of too much work aimed at standards that are too high is necessarily harmful to the worker, but it can have a chilling effect on family relationships. Under the best of conditions, spouses express concern about not having enough time with each other. When either partner spends much more time at work than at home, and obsesses about work while not on the job, the amount of time available for a marriage will hardly be sufficient. And when children are part of the picture, there isn't a chance that the work-obsessed parent will have enough time to spend in meeting the needs of the family. Delinquency, obesity, and teenage drug abuse have all been explained, in part, as adolescents' attempts to gain the attention of parents who are too preoccupied to hear gentler cries for notice. There is more sad truth than humor to many wives' wry comments about their children asking "Who's that man?" when their fathers walk through the front door.

The only way to determine whether the work pattern of a spouse or parent poses problems for the family is to openly discuss the matter. These discussions require considerable tact. Workaholics are not evil; they often consider themselves to be self-sacrificing, and they may feel unappreciated when family members complain about their absences from home. If the discussion of work begins in an accusatory way, defensiveness will prevent understanding. Agreement is more likely if the discussion begins with appreciation of the workaholic's achievement and expression of the feeling that he or she is missed by the family. The result can be a realignment of the way work and family commitments are balanced.

The Time Crunch

Most working couples want all the benefits of a two-career family—such as money, recognition, power, and personal satisfaction—and all the benefits of a traditional family—like a clean house, good meals, time together as a couple, and plenty of time with the children. In the era of the "super-woman," many working wives are trying to do it all, and most burn out before they get close to achieving their goals. Very few couples have enough time to do everything that needs to be done. Time is a limited resource, and we do not have infinite ways to "save time," so we must make choices about what will and won't get done.

Housework may seem to be a minor area of concern, but

it is usually the area of greatest conflict and dissatisfaction. Any woman who works full-time discovers that she lacks the time and energy to meet household demands singlehandedly. Wives who become mothers, and wives who move from the traditional role to working outside the home are particularly stressed by the difficulty of meeting constant demands. Most women reach the point at which they must lower their standards and redistribute household responsibilities.

There are times when all working couples have to live with dirty floors, dusty furniture, and "quick and easy" dinners. Even if husband and wife share household tasks, they often lack both the time and the desire to spend their evenings and weekends doing housework. A lot of conflict and anxiety can be avoided simply by taking a more casual approach to meals and household maintenance.

Still, no matter what standards are used, most households demand more work than can be done by one, particularly if that one works full-time. Husbands and wives must work out a plan for sharing responsibilities that each feels is fair. If there are older children in the home, parents can request that they, too, share some of the household tasks. Of course, fewer sacrifices need to be made if you can afford to hire someone to help with the housework. Household help can free both spouses from some of the less rewarding tasks, and give them time for more fulfilling endeavors.

While many couples are able to adjust some of their housekeeping standards, working parents do not want to compromise where their children are concerned. Working mothers of young children often feel guilty about being away from them at all, and they emphasize the increase in "quality time" that they count on to compensate for the smaller quantity of time they spend with their children. Most working parents quickly discover that any time left after finishing work and household tasks is taken up by the children.

After meeting the demands of work, house, and children, couples often find they have no time left. Without having made the decision to sacrifice time alone, together, or with friends, they discover that "free" time has been eliminated from their lives. This may not be a major concern while the pleasures and challenges of combining career and family are new, but problems surface eventually.

Friendships are often the first to be sacrificed. Without ever intending to lose contact with our friends, we may see them less and less often due to lack of time and difficulty coordinating schedules. But when we give up friends, we lose important sources of support. Our friends can provide us with perspective on our lives that keeps us from becoming restricted by our own narrow view. Friends also offer stimulation in areas that spouses often can't. We overburden our marriages by insisting that our spouses share all our interests, or by limiting our pleasures to those our partners enjoy. No one person can or should meet all of our needs, and friends are an important source of pleasure and companionship.

As every divorced person knows, friends are often most valuable during times of stress. When we need more support than we can get from our mates, when our mates are unavailable for any reason, or when we simply want the benefit of another point of view, we turn to our friends. Women are more apt to recognize the importance of a supportive network, but men, too, are beginning to appreciate the value of friendships. When we sacrifice our friends to other demands, we are jeopardizing our personal and marital satisfaction.

Time alone is also quickly lost to other demands. Many of us believe that solitary time is self-indulgent, and therefore not justifiable when so many other demands must be met. Women often spend so much time meeting other people's needs that they totally neglect their own. Stepparents who have never had children of their own often have trouble adjusting to the loss of private time that inevitably accompanies parenthood.

Time away from others is a necessity. Regardless of the other demands we face, we all need a chance to relax and reflect. The absence of private time can lead to an eroding sense of self and a less stimulating relationship. If we can't take time out, we can't enjoy time in.

Finally, we often find that time together as a couple is in short supply. Unfortunately, conflicts between the demands of the relationship and those of the job are often resolved in favor of work. We are more willing to say "Sorry, I'm too busy" to our spouses than to our bosses.

Working parents have even more problems. Despite their efforts to limit their working hours, parents may lose time together through an effort to stagger work times so that the children are seldom home alone. As a result, parents often find they have no time to nurture their own relationship, and this can have a devastating effect on their marriage. Relaxed time with our partners is as important as any other "demand" in our lives.

The only way to assure time to nurture ourselves, our friendships, and our marriages is to treat these activities as necessities and schedule them along with other essential activities. Some working parents actually make formal "dates" with each other. Others have standing commitments to individual and social activities that assure them identities apart from the family. However it is done, it is essential that none of these uses of time be regularly subjugated to other demands.

Establishing a Balance

There is no "best" way to redistribute the time allocated to household chores and care of the children. If both spouses are spending approximately the same number of hours at work, they should also spend similar amounts of time meeting home responsibilities. The details of the arrangement, however, must be tailored to the individuals. Every couple can work out a balance of work, family, personal, and social activities that works best for all concerned.

To reach a satisfying agreement, you should first determine how well your present arrangement is working. Then you need to make decisions about how to allocate responsibility for home and work duties. Finally, you should specify the details about how and when each task is to be accomplished.

Estimating Where You Stand Today

There are two relevant dimensions of our home and work efforts; one is finite and the other almost without limit. The limited dimension is time. There is no way to expand the 168 hour week, although we may find ways to use time more productively or more enjoyably. The virtually limitless dimension is the amount of appreciation we can express for each other's efforts. The most boring and thankless tasks can be made bearable if they produce enough acknowledgement in ways that count by people that matter. As a first step in evaluating the balance between home and work, it's helpful to determine your current satisfaction.

From answers to the questions on the next page, you will be able to determine whether change in any of these areas can be useful. You and your spouse should answer these questions separately, score and think about your own responses, and then discuss the results.

Guidelines for discussion: Start by identifying each item with which you both express satisfaction by selecting a rating of "1" or "2". Many couples agree on positive ratings for about half of the items. For each item of agreement, tell each other some of the particulars that contribute to your satisfaction.

Next, turn to the items marked "4" or "5." These are areas in which someone is dissatisfied. For each item, think of changes that might increase your satisfaction, and share the ones that can be expressed without criticism or accusation. Don't try to negotiate agreement yet, just discuss possibilities. You may also want to discuss areas placed in the "3" category, just to explore possibilities for improvement.

SATISFACTION WITH HOME/WORK BALANCE

Thinking about the past several months, and allowing for any special situations like illness or extraordinary job pressure, how satisfied have you been with each of the following aspects of your personal, family, and work activities?

	Very Satisfied				*Very Dissatisfied*
The amount of free time we have together	1	2	3	4	5
The amount of free time I have just for myself	1	2	3	4	5
The amount of housework that I am expected to do	1	2	3	4	5
The amount of housework that my spouse *actually does*	1	2	3	4	5
The amount of time I spend with our children	1	2	3	4	5
The amount of time my partner spends with our children	1	2	3	4	5
The amount of time I spend working for pay	1	2	3	4	5
The amount of time my partner spends working for pay	1	2	3	4	5

SATISFACTION WITH HOME *(Continued)*

	Very Satisfied				*Very Dissatisfied*
The amount of money we have as a family	1	2	3	4	5
The amount of support that I receive from my spouse for my:					
a. housekeeping efforts	1	2	3	4	5
b. efforts with our children	1	2	3	4	5
c. efforts to earn money	1	2	3	4	5
d. efforts to maintain friendships	1	2	3	4	5
e. self-growth efforts	1	2	3	4	5
f. efforts to spend time together	1	2	3	4	5

For some items, you may feel that change is impossible. Nevertheless, it's worth trying to find some solutions. If a careful exploration of alternatives reveals that the situation can't be changed, look for new ways to support each other's efforts to cope with a bad situation. For those areas in which changes can be made, the following exercise will provide some help in agreeing to changes.

Making Decisions

In Chapter 5 we presented a framework for allocating authority for decisions about money. Now you can use the same model for making decisions about home and work responsibilities. We'll briefly review the principles here.

Remember that no one should have authority for making a decision without the responsibility to implement it. Husbands are not free to decide that wives should vacuum the house daily. Remember, too, that no framework for decision-making is adequate unless both partners feel that it is equitable. Equity is far more important than equality. A husband may want his wife to move to a new city for his own career advancement. He may be willing to exchange the right to decide where they live for her right to make most of the other decisions. She may agree to move in exchange for the authority to decide which house they buy, which school their children attend, what job she takes, what hours she works, and so forth. In numbers, it's his one decision to her many, but in quality, both are satisfied with what they have.

Decide whether each issue is of great importance (*), moderate importance (+), or little importance (−) to you. Next, use the following scale to indicate how each of you would like to allocate responsibility for making decisions:

H: The husband decides, but offers his wife occasional veto authority.

H/w: The husband decides, but with careful consideration of his wife's opinions and preferences.

H/W: The couple shares decision making authority. In some cases they can find a mutually acceptable compromise, and in others they take turns deciding, using the H/w and W/h models in equal balance.

W/h: The wife decides, but with careful consideration of her husband's opinions and preferences.

W: The wife decides, but offers her husband occasional veto authority.

In using this scale, remember that neither you nor your partner should have absolute authority in any area, because each can be affected by every decision made by the other. Nevertheless, at the extremes of H and W, vetos should be used sparingly and only when one of you feels that your partner's actions would have a very negative impact upon you.

As an example, one spouse may want to take a job that entails long working hours, while the other may object to the time commitment the job demands. Of course the objecting partner will express an opinion, but if the decision about what job to take is in the extreme category (H or W), the spouse who will be doing the work makes the final decision. The other mate can exercise the option to cast a veto on this issue if it is extremely important. But casting a "no" vote here will entail accepting many other decisions, including some that may have a more direct impact. Therefore, vetoes must be exercised with caution and only after careful consideration.

Use the H/w and W/h categories for areas in which you are willing to entertain more discussion, bearing in mind that the person who has the responsibility for carrying out the decision still has the right to make the final decision. For example, a husband is extremely concerned about eating all-natural foods cooked from scratch, but his wife does most of the cooking. Therefore, what to eat is a W/h decision. If she shares his concern, she may be happy to do as he asks, but she may be more interested in saving time than in cooking only the healthiest foods. If she does not share his interest, she may agree to avoid certain ingredients to which he objects strongly, or she may let him make some menu decisions, or she may simply agree to keep his preferences in mind. Unless the husband is willing to do the cooking, he has a limited voice in food preparation.

Finally, the third decision-making category should be used for items about which you have equally strong feelings and shared responsibility. At times you will arrive at a decision that satisfies you both, while at other times you will agree to alternate between doing things his way and her way.

As before, you should start by doing the exercise separately. First, establish the importance you place on each area of decision making. Then assign a decision-making category to each area. Finally, compare your responses and negotiate a mutually acceptable way to make decisions in each area.

The final step is to specify in writing the details of the agreements listed above. This must be done to avoid the conflict that so often results when spouses agree to share household responsibilities. Because partners often have very different ideas about *how* a job should be carried out, they may disagree as to *whether* or not a job has been done. For example, a husband may agree to take responsibility for taking out the garbage. But whereas his wife thinks the garbage can should be emptied daily, he thinks it should go out when the lid can no longer be closed. Their different ideas of a job well done can lead to fights that could be easily avoided by agreeing on the specifics of each job. Therefore, instead of writing "Do the dishes," one might specify "Wash the dishes within an hour after each meal," or "Wash the dishes once a day." Specification thus includes what is to be done, the standards by which it is to be done, and the frequency and timing with which it is to be done.

Since a marriage is not a business, the agreement should not take the rigid form of a legal agreement. Instead, each of you should make a list of what you would like the other to do, with the realization that neither may be able to do it

ALLOCATING RESPONSIBILITY
AND AUTHORITY

Area	Importance	Authority
	*, +, −	H,Hw,HW,Wh,W
What job husband takes		
What job wife takes		
Hours husband works		
Hours wife works		
Menu planning		
Grocery shopping		
Cooking		
Dish washing		
Garbage		
Dusting		
Vacuuming		
Mopping		
Laundry		
Auto maintenance		
Yard care		
Pet care		
Paying bills		

ALLOCATING RESPONSIBILITY
AND AUTHORITY *(Continued)*

Area	Importance	Authority
Planning social activities		
Planning vacations		
Child care:		
after-school care		
evening care		
sick days		
carpooling or driving		
Other		

all on a regular basis. But as long as each does a reasonable share of agreed-upon tasks, you are both likely to be content. With luck, you may even find time to have fun after all the work is done.

9
Stepparenting

*I*f you believe the fairy tales you heard as a child, the words "good stepparent" would be a contradiction. Step roles seem to evoke a mixture of fear and pity, and the current language describing them is awkward at best. Even greeting card companies, which seldom miss a chance to make a buck, know when to stay away; it's not easy to find cards with messages like "Happy birthday beloved stepson" or "To the best second mom in all the land, with thanks for stepping in."

Little is known about how stepfamilies operate, even though they are fast becoming as numerous as traditional families. About half of the children born in America since 1970 can expect to live in stepfamilies, and many of these will experience their parents' third or fourth marriages as well. By the age of 18, most of today's children will have to hesitate before answering the question "What are your parents' names?" And as they ponder, they'll realize that they also have new relatives in roles for which no titles exist.

We know almost nothing about what stepfamilies do to

succeed or fail. There are millions of stepfamilies, but the National Institutes of Health researchers found that only 550 of them had been studied at all by 1979, and most of the research in which they participated was of poor quality. Little progress has been made since then, so we still have few facts about the dos and don'ts of stepparenting.

In most life situations, we forget about the experts and rely on our own experience as a teacher. But in the realm of stepparenting, experience lets us down. Few of today's parents lived in recombined families when they were young, and most of us still call upon our natural parents as our only parental models. But while biological parents and stepparents have important things in common, there are major differences in their roles. Failure to understand these differences can lead to unnecessary confusion when families are combined.

The myths that have grown up around stepparenting serve only to confuse and frustrate all family members. The widespread belief in these myths may prompt much of the stress and strain felt by stepparents. It's important to understand the difficulties, but instead of being paralyzed by this awareness, we can use it to develop a plan of action. With care and common sense, remarried parents can create a climate that is much more reasonable and harmonious than the mythical representation.

It's never too soon or too late to start a constructive approach to stepparenting. We'll begin by debunking six common myths about children and their new families. In doing so, we'll concentrate only on the children and their step and natural parents. Other people have a stake in the children's care: some grandparents have begun to fight for the right to maintain contact with the children, and other friends and relatives also express a desire to remain involved. These are important concerns. But the problems within the immediate family are the ones that affect the children and the remarried couple on a daily basis. So we'll concentrate on suggestions for helping these relationships run smoothly.

Myth 1   Children make marriages happier

Most of us yield to the biological drive to have children, and those who are not yet parents believe the birth of children would make their marriage happier. Unfortunately, the reverse is often true. Almost all couples become less happy with their marriages after their first child is born and they typically stay that way for as long as the children are at home.

Financial strains, role changes, and increasing workloads all contribute to this loss of marital satisfaction. But another factor is even more important. Parents derive great joy from a feeling of attachment to their children and from sharing the excitment of their development. But children demand and receive a tremendous amount of their parents' time and energy, and few parents escape occasional feelings of jealousy and neglect.

As a result, most parents complain about having less opportunity than they would like for emotional and sexual intimacy. Wives complain that they have fewer stimulating conversations with their husbands, and less opportunity for shared projects. Husbands feel that time once available for discussing their concerns has been usurped by talk of problems with the diaper service, the older child's intimidation of a younger sibling, or lost or stolen bicycles.

Most parents pin their hopes on an endless series of transition points, thinking that things will get easier as soon as the child . . . sleeps through the night . . . begins to walk . . . can ask for things rather than having to cry to get them . . . is toilet trained . . . starts preschool . . . can play outside alone for a few hours . . . starts elementary school . . . and on and on. In fact, the presence of the child is always felt. The issues change, but the demand for attention remains high for many years.

Accepting parenthood as a mixed blessing has spurred a change in attitudes toward parenting. A majority of adults now believe that parents, too, have needs that must be met. For example, many believe they should have some time and money for themselves, even if this means less time with the children and fewer dollars in their estates. Also, while it was once a foregone conclusion that parents should stay in unhappy marriages for the sake of the children, nearly two thirds of the respondents in a recent survey by Daniel Yankelovich rejected this idea. These shifts in attitude reflect acceptance of the fact that parents, too, have needs.

Stepparents who have never had children of their own usually have some trouble adjusting to parenthood. If they were childless by choice, the children of their new spouse may simply be part of the price of admission to the marriage they wanted. If the natural parent expects the new spouse to be delighted at the opportunity to be an instant parent, the marriage is going to be in trouble. Other stepparents who did not have children of their own may idealize children and consider their new mate's offspring to be a benefit of marriage rather than a cost. In their enthusiasm, they may overlook some of the difficulties of child-rearing, and they can be very disappointed when their dreams of a perfect family don't come true.

People who think parenthood should be a constant source of joy and fulfillment feel guilty and disappointed when their expectations aren't met. Those who realistically accept mixed feelings about their children's intrusions have a much easier time dealing with the realities of parenthood. Natural parents who can acknowledge the costs as well as the benefits of parenthood are in a much better position to help stepparents adjust to the demands of instant parenthood.

Myth 2   Children have about the same impact on their parents' second marriages as they did on first marriages

It's tempting to believe this, but the fact is that children from former marriages create some predictable strains in second marriages.

People marrying for the first time are usually able to adjust to each other at a leisurely pace. They start with a honeymoon and then often have a few years of living alone together before the children arrive. Not so for remarrying couples. It's not unusual for offspring of former marriages to accompany new couples on their wedding trips, if there is a wedding trip at all. Needless to say, it's difficult to get to know another person under the watchful and sometimes hostile eyes of children who are there from the very beginning.

It's hard enough for two parents to agree on how to raise children, but in second marriages, decisions about children may involve three, four, or even more adults, all of whom have strong beliefs about child-rearing. Conflicting goals and values are almost inevitable, and models for achieving harmony are nonexistent.

Stepparents and natural parents cannot help but feel differently about the children. Blood, as they say, is thicker than water. The stepparent may feel isolated by, and perhaps jealous of, a spouse's attachment to children of a first marriage. And the parent may be angry that the new spouse fails to form an equally strong attachment. If both partners bring children from previous marriages, the potential for multilateral alliances and jealousies assume the proportions of a soap opera.

Remarried families also have to do more with less. Nearly everyone emerges from divorce in a somewhat damaged financial state. With slimmer resources, these newly constructed families are expected to meet the greater needs of older children, from more expensive clothing and gas money to such "luxuries" as private phones and stereo equipment.

It's not unusual for conflicts over stepparent-child relationships to cause a second marriage to end. Therefore, whether the natural parent is a father or a mother, great tact and sensitivity will be needed to help smooth the stepparent's entry into the family. This requires something akin to a therapeutic approach in which the natural parent listens sympathetically to the stepparent's concerns, accepts rather than criticizes them, shares in planning ways to improve the stepparent's relationship with the children, and energetically helps everyone make these positive plans a reality.

Myth 3   *Children are always disturbed by their parents' divorce*

Because most of us believe in the importance of the two-parent family, we often feel that children must suffer when their parents divorce. But most researchers conclude that the adjustment and self-concepts of children whose parents divorced are either no different or even better than those of children living with both natural parents. The principal lasting effect of parental divorce seems to be an increase in the chances that the children will themselves divorce.

Children sometimes get swept up in the conflict that precedes their parents' divorce, and absorb their parents' anxiety over the prospect of separation. They may also experience some stress stemming from the economic consequences of divorce. But these usually prove to be short-term problems, and few of the children studied describe their parents' divorce as an overwhelmingly distressing experience. Dealing with the need to form relationships with parents separately seems easier for the child than having to adjust to parents who are constantly at each other's throats.

All too often, though, parents feel guilty and try to compensate their children for imagined hurts. This leads some parents to rush into second marriages to restore the children to a two-parent home. Even when the decision to remarry is a wise one, natural parents may demand that stepparents bend over backward to compensate children for suffering that never took place.

Just as spouses form secret contracts during courtship, so, too, there are hidden agreements between stepparents and their new children. If the remarried couple is overly generous at the start, the child will regard this as a promise of things to come and feel resentment when the promise is not kept. Therefore, after a few "getting to know you" treats, stepparents do well to begin relating to their new children pretty much as they plan to relate to them over time.

Myth 4 *Stepparents and stepchildren should instantly love each other*

After divorce, children often have the opportunity to develop closer relationships with each of their parents. When a parent remarries, much of the attention once given to the children is focused, instead, on the new spouse.

In addition to giving up some of their new-found intimacy with a divorced parent, children are asked to make other major adjustments when a parent remarries. They are expected to stop hoping for the reunion of their natural parents. They may be forced to assume a new position in the family if the stepparent brings children from a prior marriage. For example, a child who was the youngest may have to give up the position of "baby" of the family. Most difficult of all, the children are asked to accept as a parent an adult who is a relative stranger.

Each child has a history unknown to the stepparent. Each has special ways of saying and doing things that the interloper doesn't understand. Each fears that the stepparent will try to interfere with previously established loyalties. It's no wonder that most children greet their parent's new spouse with more than a little ambivalence.

Stepparents are also thrust into situations that invite ambivalence. For them, a spouse's children from a former marriage are not "ours," but "his" or "hers." The children often have different last names, and they seldom call the stepparent "Mom" or "Dad." Since our feelings are influenced by our words, even the language of stepparenting creates emotional distance.

But much more important than the words are the mixed feelings that many stepparents bring to their new role. As mentioned earlier, stepparents without children of their own may be unpleasantly surprised at the difficulty of living with

kids. And stepparents who have lost custody of their own
children may feel guilty that they are no longer nurturing
their own children, and resentful at having to put their effort
into raising someone else's kids. Finally, all but the most
thick-skinned stepparents are sensitive to the child's ambivalence. Even those who are entirely committed to loving their
stepchildren will be slowed a bit by the children's obvious
reserve.

Natural parents may also be part of the problem. Some are
reluctant to have their new spouses establish a good relationship with their children. Those who used the children as
allies in conflicts with their first mates, or those who had to
fight for custody, may feel very possessive of the children and
resent efforts of their new spouse to get too close to them. If
a natural parent feels jealous when stepparent and children
seem very close, or insists on sharpening the distinction between *step*parent and *real* parent, a difficult job will be made
still harder.

Too much encouragement can be as harmful as too little.
Even when their motives are pure, natural parents who pressure stepparents to feel and display instant love can cause
guilt that can only interfere with positive feelings. A "love
me, love my children" approach can force a stepparent to
find fault with the child in order to justify a failure to feel
love. When this happens, everyone in the family suffers.

Even though we know that stepparents are not "real"
parents, we want them to have the same biological instincts
that natural parents do. We expect them to love their new
spouse's children as their own without the opportunity to
develop gradually the knowledge and trust upon which love
depends.

Before stepparents and children can possibly establish a
loving relationship, they need to learn a great deal about each
other. They need the time to develop a special style for their
relationship that fits in well with all existing relationships.
For example, a child may not accept her stepfather until she
is reassured that this new man is not trying to replace her

natural father. It takes time for issues like these to be resolved, and all members of combined families should expect a relaxed period of friendship to precede love between stepparents and children. If unforced, friendship will lead to the understanding and respect that set the stage for love.

Myth 5   *Children who live in two homes are worse off than children who live full-time in one home*

It is commonly believed that children who move back and forth between their parents' homes suffer special disadvantages. This belief, coupled with the common assumption that mothers are more willing and able parents than fathers, accounts for the fact that until recently some 90 percent of all contested custody decisions were decided in the mother's favor. But the tide of judicial decision-making has made a dramatic turn in the past ten years. In response to a growing number of requests for custody filed by fathers, over half the states have already passed laws that remove gender of the parent as a criterion for custody awards.

As a result of these legal changes, custody is now awarded according to the best interests of the child. The children's views are often taken into consideration and the awards may be subject to periodic review. This frees children from the pain of being caught up in custody disputes in which they often serve as pawns; the battles have more to do with money and their parents' anger toward one another than with their loving care.

But it also means that an increasing number of children are living out of suitcases as they regularly move their clothes, books, and favorite toys between their divorced parents' homes.

Joint custody is certainly no panacea. If a father was disinterested in his children before divorce, granting him joint custody will not suddenly manufacture his commitment to his children. If spouses were unable to agree about how to manage their children while married, the stress of divorce is not likely to change things for the better. And if children remain the third point in a continuing triangular argument between their parents, they will never be able to relax and adjust to the new arrangement. Yet despite arguments that joint custody is detrimental to the best interests of the child, most joint custody arrangements work reasonably well.

After remarriage, custody issues may emerge again. The first parent to remarry may feel the children are better off in the two-adult household. The other parent may feel the children shouldn't have to make yet another adjustment. When the new spouse brings children from a prior marriage, parents may disagree about the best living arrangement for all concerned.

The "best" living arrangement varies with each family. Couples differ in their interest in caring for children, in their financial ability to do so, and in other aspects of their living and work situations that can affect the quality of the home life they can offer children. On the assumption that both natural parents want to have contact with their children, and both are able to do so, we believe that the children's moving between two homes can meet everyone's needs well.

There are several advantages to having the children live part-time with each parent. The most important is that children are able to maintain close contact with both parents. And during the time they are in each home, they are likely to get more attention than they would get if they lived in either home full-time. If stepparents are actively involved, children may also gain the advantage of the broadened perspective and network of support that comes from being nurtured by more than two adults. Parents also benefit from joint custody, since it gives them the opportunity to reestablish intimacy in their new relationships while the children are in their other home.

Rather than being a liability, children's moving between two households can work to everyone's advantage. It will work best if the homes are not too far apart, and if the children can have an appropriate amount of personal space in each. And it can only work well if all of the adults and children cooperate in sensitively working out the many complicated details of the arrangment.

Myth 6   There is one right way to raise children

Before remarrying, we discuss whether we will have a family with our new spouse, but we almost never discuss the details of child-rearing. Our secret contract usually includes the expectation that our new spouse will want to raise children exactly as we would.

Whether or not we are parents, we all bring beliefs about child-rearing to our new marriages. Even if we have never put them into words, many of these beliefs are core elements in the way we think about life, so they are far more than casual concerns.

If partners view most child-rearing issues similarly, or if they are successful in developing a shared point of view, parenting, and their marriage, can be smooth and relatively easy. But when differences are unresolved, problems are unavoidable. Parents of troubled children differ from those whose children do well not as much in their method of child-rearing as in the level of consistency with which they approach their children. A study comparing families with delinquent children and families with children who did well revealed that it didn't matter whether parents were permissive or authoritarian as long as they both agreed about how to raise children.

When parents agree on philosophy, they approach their children with consistency. When they disagree, the children become confused and uncertain. To reduce uncertainty, children often either test the system by going to extremes in order to see how the adults will behave, or they try to play one adult against the other. If the child is successful in placing a wedge between natural parent and stepparent, the new marriage is under stress. So strong agreement about how to deal with the children works to the advantage of everyone in the family.

Among remarried couples, disagreements about the children are often a major source of stress. More than one second marriage has broken down over conflicts about how restrictive or permissive parents should be, whether children should be given or expected to earn their spending money, when and under what circumstances adolescents should be allowed to date, and hundreds of other details.

Many natural parents experience their new spouses' criticisms about child-rearing as a personal attack or as a rejection of the child. Even if the natural parent has said exactly the same thing on other occasions, hearing it from a stepparent can be taken as a call to arms. The natural parent may also disregard the stepparent's criticism, feeling that the new spouse doesn't know the child well enough to make judgments. The stepparent, on the other hand, can claim the ability to be more objective about the children, and to offer a different point of view worthy of consideration.

Both natural and stepparents make good points. It's important to know the child's history, but it's also important to have a fresh perspective. Both therefore have something important to contribute to the development of a child management strategy. If either parent claims insight into the "one true way," the chance for discussion is lost, and everyone suffers. Therefore every remarrying couple should come to an agreement about how to rear their children, and the best arrangement is likely to be an amalgam of both views.

A Constructive Approach to Stepparenting

It's important to keep in mind that much of what happens when stepfamilies first come together is strongly influenced by the recent past. Loss of contact with a spouse or parent, loss of familiar and satisfying roles, the need to take on new relationships and responsibilities, and difficulties adjusting to physical and economic changes all contribute to the uncertainty, insecurity, and hypersensitivity of all concerned. Initial reactions of all stepfamily members have more to do with the past than the present. Therefore, we must try not to overreact when things don't go as expected, and have confidence that with patience and understanding they will improve.

Progress can be hastened, however, by understanding some of the most common challenges faced by stepfamilies, and planning ways to successfully meet those challenges. As we have emphasized throughout this book, everyone should know as much as possible about what is expected of them. An awareness of expectations keeps unpleasant surprises to a minimum, and reduces the likelihood of impulsive and ineffective reactions to unanticipated situations.

We have also stressed that rights and responsibilities must go hand-in-hand. It's very easy for each parent to make decisions about how the other should act with the children. A mother might decide that the father should be the disciplinarian (in which case she's the judge and he's the executioner) or a father might decide that the mother should take the children to a wide variety of time-consuming after-school activities (in which case he's the decision-maker and she's the implementer). These arrangements generally breed resentment and inefficiency. As is the case with work, money, and household decision-making, the right to make decisions involving children belongs to the person who has the responsibility and authority for implementing those decisions.

Let's turn now to specific issues of concern to members of combined families. While not every remarried couple will experience difficulty in all of these areas, these concerns were among those that the National Institute of Mental Health researchers identified as the most common sources of confusion and stress for reformed families.

Names

The language of stepparenting is a quagmire. It is probably important for the child to differentiate between his stepparent and his biological one. But it is extremely awkward for a child to call his mother's new husband "Stepdaddy," and it is confusing for a child to call two men "Dad." And for teenagers, it's difficult enough to have one father and mother; to have two of either adds insult to injury.

Many people find an adequate solution by choosing to use first names. While some adults may feel a little uncomfortable when a child calls them by name, use of first names is comfortably familiar and eliminates confusion. When one father came home with a much younger wife, his teenage son asked: "How can I call a woman who likes the same music I do, 'Mother'?" The father replied "You have only one mother. My new wife's name is Paula, and I hope that's what you'll call her."

Both parent and stepparent should agree on what they would like the children to call the stepparent. If the children are old enough, they should be consulted and asked if they have a preference. If their other parent still plays a role in their lives, and if the children don't have a clear preference to the contrary, it's usually easiest for everyone to call each other by first name. That way, there is never an implied breach of respect for the divorced parent, no one appears to be usurping the role of mother or father, and there's no hint of an attempt to delude the child.

Parental Authority

In stepfamilies, it's often unclear who has the ultimate child-rearing authority. Since remarrying partners seldom discuss the distribution of power and responsibility in child-rearing, a pattern just evolves. Unfortunately, many couples are not happy with the model they end up using.

In too many combined families, partners share child-rearing responsibilities fairly equally, but the biological parent retains the ultimate decision-making authority. This has some very negative implications. If the stepparent doesn't have equal authority, he or she is stuck having responsibility without power. This can lead not only to hostility and resentment between spouses, but it also results in less effective parenting. Therefore, it is unreasonable to expect a stepparent to assume child-rearing responsibility in areas where he or she does not have authority.

Using this assumption as a guideline for allocating responsibility, a remarried couple can work out an arrangement acceptable to both. Some couples are eager to have the stepparent share all parenting responsibilities, in which case the stepparent should also have equal authority in every realm of decision-making. Other couples are happy to have the biological parent retain most of the authority and responsibility. In this case, a clear distinction between parent and stepparent is accepted by all.

When both partners agree on the roles they want to take, allocating authority is easy. But frequently, spouses have different expectations of the parenting roles that each will assume. Some parents want the stepparents to assume more of a parenting role than the stepparents feel comfortable taking. Other parents feel their new spouses are assuming more parental power than they are willing to relinquish.

There is no "best" way to allocate power between parent and stepparent. You should discuss your desires and expectations, and compromise until you both are comfortable. If either of you is hesitant about having the stepparent take on too much authority or responsibility at the beginning, the transition should be made slowly.

To structure your discussion, the form on pages 181–82 may be helpful. First, determine which areas are important to each of you, by using $(+)$ for very important, (0) for neutral, and $(-)$ for unimportant. Pay close attention to this evaluation. If you can agree on the importance of each area, you can develop a shared set of values for managing children. This can cut down on fights that develop when one spouse feels the other is neglecting important concerns.

Next, you should agree about who is most likely to have responsibility for supervising follow-through in each area (F-father, M-mother). It's only fair that the person who is expected to put time and effort into helping the child achieve a goal should have a large role in determining the objective.

Finally, you are ready to decide who should have authority for making each decision (F-father, M-mother, C-child). Because so many people are involved, allocating authority for making decisions about children in combined families is more complex than are other areas of decision-making. If the children are living in two homes, the natural parent might want to consider the attitudes of the children's other parent when determining importantance of various goals in order to achieve consistency. Complete consistency is an elusive goal, but children do better when not asked to decide for themselves which parent's directions to follow.

This form also includes space for allowing the children to have some authority for decisions that affect them. Older children will naturally have more authority, but you may agree that even younger children should have a voice in making some of the decisions that affect them. For each item, any combination of father, mother, and child is fine.

Because different areas of decision-making are relevant to children of varied ages, we ask that you supplement this list with items relevant to your family. You may even decide to use a different copy of this form for children of different ages. As before, we ask that you use this form to identify your own preferences before using it to reach agreement about a pattern of decision-making acceptable to parents and children alike.

CHILD MANAGEMENT DECISION-MAKING

Area	How important? + 0 −	Who responsible? F M	Who Decides? F M C
Bedtime or curfew			
Keeping own things neat			
Keeping family space neat			
Allowance			
Part-time jobs			
Clothes (style)			
Education Where Standards			
Religious activity			
Use of phone			
Use of stereo, TV			
Use of car			
Dating			
Respect for parents			

CHILD MANAGEMENT *(Continued)*

Area	How important? + 0 −	Who responsible? F M	Who Decides? F M C
Behavior toward siblings			
Choice of Friends			
Use of alcohol			
Use of drugs			
Recreation Which activities How often			
Other			

Managing Daily Routines

The goals parents set for children have a great effect on the daily decisions that must be made. But when stepparents join families, they are often expected to live with and even enforce decisions they had no part in making. Any attempt to change the status quo leads to a feeling of walking on eggs.

This was the situation for Dick and his second wife Barbara. In Dick's first marriage, he and his wife realized that they could not have complete control of their children's behavior, so they decided to concentrate their energies on helping their children to be healthy, kind, and smart. They decided not to worry about making them neat, competitive, or great musicians, among other things. By the time they were teenagers, the children ate healthy foods and drove defensively, they were considerate to everyone but each other, and they did very well in school. But they were terribly messy, reluctantly entered competitive activities, and were totally lacking in musical talent.

Years after Dick and his first wife divorced, Barbara entered a household in which she found children who were smart, healthy slobs. Their bedroom floors were an obstacle course, the bathroom a disaster area, and their belongings were conspicuous everywhere in the house. She was much less interested in their unusual health behavior profile and their high grades than in the fact that they made her living space a shambles.

Dick and Barbara had three options for dealing with a situation in which he was content with the way things were going and she was disgusted. They could agree to keep things as they were, leaving Barbara to grin and bear it or wander through the house making sarcastic remarks; they could tell the children to start to live up to a new set of standards; or they could sit down together and negotiate a mutually acceptable way of doing things.

As most stepparents do, Barbara initially kept silent about her concerns and tried to adjust to the situation. But she grew increasingly upset as the garbage and clutter mounted. Then she tried to intervene directly, only to find the children agreeing but failing to follow through. When she was sufficiently frustrated, she angrily presented the problem to Dick, who felt she was attacking him for the way he was raising his children.

Because people can't be expected to give enthusiastic support to decisions they had no part in making, Dick, like all remarrying parents, should have discussed with Barbara his values and goals where the children were concerned. After understanding the logic of his approach, she might have accepted and supported some aspects, and requested changes in others. As always, disagreements should be resolved in favor of the person who has the responsibility. For example, if Dick is happy to help the children with their homework, he can set doing well in school as a high-priority goal; if Barbara does most of the housework, she has a right to demand that the children clean up their act.

Children should not be expected to make massive adjustments as soon as a stepparent arrives, so stepparents should be careful to limit the changes requested to those they consider to be most important. We suggest this three-step program for making needed changes.

1. Evaluate the way you feel important routines are being handled—everything from how children maintain their bedrooms to how respectfully they treat others in the family.

2. Discuss your evaluations, agreeing about which routines are now running smoothly and what changes would make others run as well.

3. Then involve the children in a discussion of areas of change. Be sure you state the reason for the request (e.g., "Judy can't sleep if the stereo is too loud, so how can we arrange to play it softly after 10 P.M.") so that your requests do not appear to be arbitrary. Also be certain that you ask for and listen to each child's suggestion for ways to get the job done. They are more likely to cooperate in changes they helped to plan.

Having these discussions early in a new marriage, and returning to them periodically in the spirit of a "State Of Our Family" review, can go far toward preventing the buildup of resentments that grow harder to resolve over time.

What To Praise and Punish

After you both agree on how you want the children to behave, your next task is to decide what each of you can do to achieve the desired behaviors. You should be certain that your list of goals is short enough so that you can pay attention to each detail and respond as needed to each behavior. You should also agree which behaviors you will praise, punish, or ignore.

Be careful not to establish more goals than you are both willing and able to monitor and reinforce. Otherwise, children will not take the goals seriously. Many parents make the mistake of formulating so many goals that they are unable to provide the reinforcement needed by any of them. They turn to a "brush fire" strategy in which they ignore the goal until it seems to be totally neglected by the child, then they either promise rewards for compliance or threaten severe punishments for noncompliance. That leads to frustration for the parent and behavioral inconsistency on the part of the child.

As an example, most parents want their children to do their homework and many have specific expectations about when, where, and how their children should study. One couple expected their children to do their homework between 4:30 and 6:00 P.M., and 7:15 and 10:00 P.M. every school day. "Study for the next exam" was their often given reply to the frequent "I did my homework during study hall in school today." They expected their children to sit at their desks to study. "I have to sit all day at school" was greeted with "You can't concentrate lying down." They expected the radio to be off during homework hours. The children's "I think better with my music on" was discounted out of hand. The list was so long that it was oppressive and added much bitterness to the already distasteful homework pill. And it forced the children to pay attention to details that were clearly irrelevant to the task at hand. The children never got to school without their homework neatly done, and they never got an A.

It's important to keep the number of rules to a minimum. Remember that in order to enforce a rule, you have to be able to pay attention to the relevant behavior and respond appropriately to each action. Parents who make rules about how

their children should do their homework must be on hand
to monitor the process, while those who just insist that homework be completed can be content with looking over the end
result. Therefore, rules should be focused on outcomes, not
on the process through which the goals are to be achieved.

While remarrying parents have many issues to resolve
concerning goals for their children, most conflict is over the
way they think these goals should be met. It is kinder to all
concerned if they will agree that homework should be done,
bathrooms left neat, and beds made, allowing the children to
decide how the goals are to be accomplished.

After you have agreed to focus on outcomes instead of
process, you have achieved freedom from having to pay attention to hundreds of details. But you still have another
decision to make: should you concentrate on praising good
results or punishing poor ones?

Praise is by far the most effective tactic to use in families.
As we said earlier, we all depend on our families to help us
feel good about ourselves. Praise creates these good feelings
and therefore strengthens bonds between all family members. Punishment poses many problems. If it is severe and
immediate, it can lead to a rapid change in behavior. But
problem behaviors recur when the angry parent is not
around, punishment creates avoidance of the parent, and
punishment teaches what *not* to do rather than offering guid-
ance about desired behavior.

How can we control our children's behavior without punishment? We can rely heavily on rewarding the things we
like. The best reward that we can offer is free; it's caring
attention. We will all move mountains if rewarded with attention from important people. Beyond attention, extra
privileges work very well. For example, a few minutes' delay
of bedtime is a powerful inducement for young children, and
the use of a car can do wonders for teenagers.

In many stepfamilies, one parent usually dispenses the
rewards while the other metes out punishment. The stepparent might be the one who is rewarding as a way of winning

favor with the children. But stepparents may also arrive with their heavy cannons in an attempt to quickly revamp child-management tactics of which they don't approve. Natural parents who depended on their children for closeness after divorce may continue to be nurturant toward the children when they remarry. Or natural parents may suddenly set severe limits to make sure the children don't cause problems for the stepparent. Any of these things can happen, and all can cause problems.

We have already stressed the importance of agreeing about the goals you have for the children. Consensus is also important in deciding what to reward and punish. You should agree on a long list of behaviors that both of you will praise, and a much shorter list of things you both will punish. With parent and stepparent sharing in the creation of strategies (rules) and tactics (praise and punishment), you can both enjoy the children's love and respect.

Different Rules in Different Homes

Whenever children spend time in two different households, they are likely to face two different sets of expectations, and some parents worry that inconsistencies between households will cause problems for the children. The potential for confusion certainly exists, but the adults in both households can work together to prevent problems. First, children must know exactly what is expected of them in Mom's and Dad's house. They can learn to live with different rules in different homes as easily as they adjust to different rules at home and in school. But *it is crucial that parents respect and never undermine the rules and expectations set forth in each other's home.*

It's very easy for us to decide that our rules are fair, and those used by a former spouse are unreasonable. If we act on this belief, we won't change the other parent, we'll only provoke anger. We will also set a precedent for the children to be disrespectful, not only of the other parent but of our own rules as well. Therefore, it's essential that we offer the same support of the other parent's rules that we would like to receive.

Support does not mean agreement. One parent may want the children to be in bed by 10 P.M. The other may be happy to let them stay up as late as they please, as long as they are not tired the next day. The 10-o'clock parent and the stay-up parent could call each other "irresponsible" or "uptight," but they would be starting a war in which everyone would lose.

Time With Children

As mentioned earlier, having children always reduces the amount of time parents have to spend with each other. The problem can be more acute when the children live with remarried parents. Before the divorce, parents probably felt entitled to some time alone. After divorce, guilt may cause parents to give their children as much time as possible, even if it means having no free time for themselves. When they remarry, parents face a further dilemma. They want to make sure their children don't feel slighted, but they also don't want to neglect their new spouse. In an attempt to please everyone, they may insist that the new family does everything as a group.

This constant togetherness has two disadvantages. It greatly reduces opportunities for intimacy between the adults, and it forces the children to deal with two adults when one might be all that is desired.

To prevent misguided attempts to homogenize the family, parents and children can benefit by discussing their use of time. The family should arrange some time each week for:

1. Parents to be alone without the children
2. Each child to be alone with a parent or stepparent
3. Family to be together

The time together does not have to be vast, since a great deal of comfort and support can be expressed in a short time. Within reason, the time should be predictable, and protected from loss due to other pressures. This time together should be made part of the daily or weekly business, and it should be treated as a serious commitment.

Each pair of family members will elect to spend their time together differently. They might watch a TV show together, take a walk, play a game, talk seriously, or just hang out. No one should dictate how the time is spent, and each should try to make the time mutually enjoyable.

It's all too easy for a natural mother to feel that her son has lacked the stimulation of a father for a few years, and that her new husband should spend time building radios or playing baseball with the boy. But doing either of these things can feel forced to stepfather and son alike, while watching adventure shows on TV may be a much more satisfying and bonding way for both to spend an hour together. The mother can suggest other activities, but the choice should always be left to her husband and son, who will find the formula that works best for them. What people actually like is far more important than what someone else thinks they should enjoy.

Respecting Boundaries

Everyone involved in a combined family has a unique identity and a set of personal routines. Because of these differences, second marriage never affects two people in the same way. At the beginning, the stepparent and children know little about each other, and early in their relationship they must learn about each other's boundaries.

We all differ in our willingness to discuss our activities and feelings. We don't all have the same readiness to share our possessions and living space. And while some people feel frustrated when they can't offer and receive a great deal of

affection, others feel uncomfortable when they are expected
to be demonstrative. Any time that the boundaries are inad-
vertently crossed, either by moving too close or staying too
far away, we run the risk of offending.

We differ not only in the amount of privacy and openness
we want, but also in the timing and style of our privacy
needs. For example, when a daughter is happy with her
boyfriend, she may regard any question about her relationship as intrusive inquisitiveness. But when things go poorly,
she may be eager to talk about her problems and get support
or advice (which, however, she should never be expected to
follow).

Over time, parents in first marriages and their children
learn each other's preferences, and manage to coexist without constantly offending each other. But when a parent remarries, the standards for privacy and openness are likely to
change. While it may have been acceptable for children to
walk into their single parent's bedroom unannounced, this is
unlikely to be acceptable after the parent shares a bedroom
with a new spouse. Parents will probably ask for more mod-
esty from children of their own sex who are in the habit of
walking around the house in their underwear. And intimate
details that were once easily discussed at the dinner table
may have to be reserved for private bedtime conversations.

Because stepparents and their new children are completely
unaware of each other's limits, they will often be surprised
when innocent or positive intentions are met with negative
reactions. Asking a personal question or interrupting a
phone conversation may be viewed as a trivial event or a
major transgression, depending on a person's feelings about
privacy.

As always, the best way for families to deal with these
individual differences is to discuss them openly. When family
members are able to specify some of their desires about openness and privacy, they can eliminate some of the painful trial
and error.

The wish for closeness or distance varies over time. Be-

cause feelings of respect and caring are implicit in the way
we react to each other's boundaries, it's important that we
remain sensitive to shifts in each person's desire for closeness
or privacy.

Answers to the questions below can give you a sense of the
current boundaries of each family member.

1.   Which areas are not to be entered by others without
permission? Does an open door mean anyone can enter?
Does a closed door mean no one should enter?
2.   Under what circumstances may other family members
use your belongings? What about opening your mail?
3.   What areas of your personal life are not open to questions from other family members?
4.   Under what circumstances do you prefer to be left
alone? Is there any time of the day or week that you want
as "private time?"
5.   What other forms of privacy would you like?

Chores and Allowance

Like adults, most children want some money of their own,
and are often expected to earn it. Two of the issues that
confront all parents are how many household duties to assign
to the children and whether to give them money in the form
of allowance or as payment for jobs well done.

Some parents assume that maintaining the household is an
adult job, and believe it is unfair to ask children of any age
to share it. Others feel that children never do anything well,
and that it takes more effort to ride herd on them than to do
the jobs themselves. Therefore they make only token efforts
to get their children's help.

Other parents believe that children should learn to take
some responsibility for themselves as soon as they are old
enough to handle it. They also feel each child should contribute in some way to the maintenance of the household. These
parents will give children more chores and responsibilities.

Parents also have different ideas about children and money. Some parents feel their children are entitled to have money with no strings. They feel that providing pocket money is one of their obligations to their children. Some give a weekly allowance while others give money whenever their children request it.

Other parents believe that children should earn the money that they spend in order to learn responsibility, and as a means of preparing them for the realities of adult life. They pay their children for chores, babysitting, or other work, rather than giving them a regular allowance.

Patterns that were established in the first marriage or during the period following divorce are often presented as a *fait accompli* to the stepparent entering the family. But stepparents have beliefs about money that are as strong and as worthy of consideration as those of natural parents. After all, the stepparent now lives with the children and shares responsibility for them. Most stepparents perform household tasks and contribute some money to the household; they also share parenting responsibilities, including the monitoring of activities and the enforcement of rules. Therefore, money and jobs given to the children can't help but affect the stepparent, and stepparents deserve a voice in these decisions.

In this, as in virtually every other area of child-management, there are no rights and wrongs. Rules may change in accord with ups and downs in the parent's economic position, the children's capabilities and financial needs, and the amount of work that has to be done. The stepparent's entry into the family is certainly an ideal time to consider changes in any of these arrangements.

Recognizing that each family needs its own set of rules, we suggest the following as only very general guidelines.

1.   Every child should have at least some responsibility for maintaining his or her room, as well as having the job of keeping track of personal property in the rest of the house.

2. Every child should have at least some minor responsibility for keeping up the household.

3. Every child should receive some allowance, as well as have the opportunity to earn some additional money if family finances permit. Because of the powerful symbolic meaning of money, it is as essential for parent and stepparent to agree on its use with the children as it is for them to agree on their own use of money. Natural parents are sometimes defensive when stepparents suggest that they give their children less, just as stepparents sometimes resent the natural parents' suggestion that the children be given more. In bargaining over the relatively small amounts of money involved in allowances and payment for chores, it's best to base your decisions on the interests of the children, rather than on the symbolic meanings of the money.

Combining Two Sets of Children

As difficult as it is to integrate one set of children into a new marriage, it's much, much harder to combine children from two families. Not only is everyone faced with all the challenges already discussed, but every obstacle is greater because of the increased number of different backgrounds, habits, expectations, daily living patterns, and family connections.

Although the task of blending two sets of children into a new and unified family may seem impossible, the methods are no different from the ones already discussed. The process may be more complex, and success may not come as quickly, but a successful blending of two families is certainly achievable. The following are just some of the challenges you face, along with some suggestions for meeting them.

It is to be expected that natural parents will be protective of their own children's interests. It is also normal for the two sets of children to fight as a means of working out their places in the new family. All too often, parents intervene to protect their natural children. Instead, when squabbles arise among the children, parents should, in the presence of the children, flip a coin to decide which parent will represent which child. As long as their advocacy is clearly random, they can avoid overidentification with their own children, and they can prevent their children from feeling "sold out" if they support the children of their mate.

Step-siblings will often resent each other and battle for power in the new family situation. Children who were eldest or youngest in their own families may find themselves in confusing new positions in their combined families. The most difficult issue concerns the responsibilities and prerogatives of the eldest. Older children are often asked to tend their younger siblings. They are also expected to make concessions when conflict arises because "they should know better." On the other hand, they usually enjoy the freedom that comes with age, and are treated more as equals by their parents.

After families have merged, the older children should not be asked to assume responsibility for the younger children of their stepparent unless they ask to do so and are rewarded for their effort. It's also important to be certain that the eldest child does not lose any privileges as a result of the new marriage—a possibility if the stepparent has different ideas about child-rearing. And it's important to be sure that the eldest child does not lose his or her seat in the Privy Council of the family. A loss in position as a parent's confidante following a parent's remarriage can be a very painful experience for a child.

Quite often, the combined family will find there just isn't enough to go around: not enough room, not enough money, not enough time, and not enough attention. Children who had their own rooms might be asked to share their living space with a new stepsister or brother. Those who formerly had their pick of new clothes might be asked to wear hand-me-downs. And those who had long private talks with their parent in the evening might have to count on trying to catch the parent's attention for a few minutes in a crowded kitchen.

We all hope that losses like these are offset by the gains of a return to traditional family living. But from the children's point of view, the immediate losses are felt far more acutely than the potential long-term gains. The losses can be ameliorated if the children are included in the process of deciding how the limited resources, whatever they are, should be shared. Using a "Family Council" to decide how to distribute limited living space, money, and parental time will allow the children to understand the logic of the changes. At the meeting, it's a good idea to begin by recognizing the importance of allowing each child to have some money, some privacy, and some private time with *both* parents. Knowing that their rights are accepted in principle can make it much easier for the children to accept a cut in their resources.

It's easy to feel overwhelmed by these and other challenges in combining families. But here, as everywhere else in the process of making remarriage work, it's essential to treat each issue separately as a problem to be solved, avoiding a natural tendency to group the problems together and regard them as a catastrophe. When you take the time to understand each other's perspective, and to respect the children's needs, you can create a combined family that is an exciting new source of support and stimulation for everyone.

Former Spouses

When parents divorce, their relationship doesn't end, it just changes. Because they share children, continued contact is necessary. Since the ex-spouse so often plays a role in a second marriage, no discussion of combined families is complete without reference to these physically absent but emotionally powerful members of the family.

Ex-spouses are often a source of stress for remarried couples. Much of the aggravation comes from continuing disputes about money. Regardless of the details of a child-support arrangement, most divorced parents feel their ex-spouse is contributing too little money or using money poorly. Second wives may feel that the ex-wife is responsible for economic hardship in the second family. Second husbands may feel that the first husband isn't doing his share to support his own children. Both partners in second marriages are likely to resent the fact that they must continue to have dealings with ex-spouses.

The very worst thing divorced parents can do is involve the children in their conflicts. Children are frequently asked to convey nasty messages between their parents, or to take sides in parental battles. Not only does this escalate conflict, but it can have a devastating effect on the children. Kids need to be free to love and respect both parents, without interference from either one. As tempting as it may be to inform children of their other parent's evil ways, it must be avoided at all costs.

While some second marriages are negatively affected by hostilities between ex-spouses, others suffer when the relationship between the former spouses is too good. Feelings of jealousy can have a very damaging effect on a second marriage. Jealous spouses can't help but be disturbed at the constant reminders that their new partner was married to and had children with someone else. They might even fear that fond memories might motivate an attempt to try again.

Very often, second spouses have difficulty openly discussing first spouses. We may be hesitant to criticize our partner's former choice, or we may be defensive about our own former choice. Yet open discussion is a necessity. First, everyone can use some reassurance that the present relationship is much better than the former one. It's also necessary to discuss feelings of jealousy so that something can be done to minimize those feelings. Usually, it's not hard to alter behaviors that provoke jealousy. For example, one woman's new husband is understandably uneasy when she has two-hour lunches with her ex-husband to discuss the children's progress in school. These discussions can just as easily take place in a more neutral location with all three adults participating.

No question about it, stepparents are confronted with

what is at best an awkward situation: the person they've married will continue to have contact with a former lover (*sic* former spouse) for many years to come. These contacts about children, money, or other shared concerns cannot fail to generate some discomfort, and it is far wiser to recognize it and discuss it than to try to pretend that it does not exist.

Rather than expecting stepparenting to be effortless, we must accept the fact that all relationships take work, and considerable effort may be needed to make second families work. Despite our knowledge of potential problems, however, a positive attitude will help us avoid self-fulfilling prophecies. We also have to allow things to develop slowly, and rather than insisting on the "right" way to handle any situation, we should adapt to circumstances as they arise. In short, there are four keys to effective stepparenting:

1. Realism
2. Optimism
3. Patience
4. Flexibility and Openness

We must keep in mind that there are no universal formulas for stepparenting, but only a vague set of notions about what might or might not work. The recommendations offered here can be used to create some tentative guidelines for making your second family work.

As a final note, stepparents and remarried parents should keep in mind that every family faces occasional problems. It's easy to attribute difficulties to the step situation. But the success of a family does not depend on whether both partners are genetically connected to the children; it depends instead on how well they function together as caring parents, how well they understand their children's perspective, and how committed they are to help their new family live at the crest of its potential.

10
Inside Assets: Outside Threats

*P*eople who marry for the second time usually know that extramarital sex is not something that happens only to other people. Infidelity is the most commonly cited reason for divorce today.

Many remarried men and women have had one or more affairs during their first marriages, or were married to a spouse who had an affair. Regardless of the details, affairs during first marriages cast long shadows over the relationships that follow. In such cases, some degree of uneasiness about infidelity is bound to carry over to a second marriage.

As most of us know, the best predictor of the way people will behave in the future is the way they acted in the past. A partner who has been unfaithful before is a likely candidate for a repeat performance during a period of marital stress. And if a wife or husband in a new couple was once married to a partner who was unfaithful, the hurt of the past may lead to suspicions that erode trust in the new marriage.

Some partners are so determined not to be hurt and humiliated again that they may start an affair simply to guard against the possibility of being left in the lurch. And the problem may be even more acute if the present spouses had been lovers while either was married to someone else. Both must cope with the realization that extramarital sex was acceptable to the other in the past, and could be chosen again.

In first marriages, some people believe their relationships are invulnerable to any threat of infidelity. Others are so frightened by the thought of it that they deny its possibility. Although it's lethal to obsess about extramarital sex, it is useful to understand not only its causes but its prevalence and effects. Through awareness, we're better equipped to prevent it from undermining trust and intimacy in second marriages.

Understanding Extramarital Sex

The words we use when we talk about extramarital sex indicate different attitudes. The terms "adultery," "infidelity," "open marriage", and even "intimate networking" have all been in vogue from time to time, and each places the behavior in a specific moral climate.

In most religions, "adultery" is forbidden and constitutes a sin, though the taboo was established mainly to protect the purity of the family's bloodline. Traditionally, we have considered it wrong for married people to have sex with anyone except a spouse. The codes of secular law usually reflect this, and even in states with no-fault divorce laws, divorces are still granted on grounds of adultery.

The term "open marriage," while not always referring primarily to sex, usually means that the partners grant each other the freedom to have sex with other people. Couples who use the phrase "intimate networking" go well beyond open marriages; they agree to participate in mate swapping, group sex, or even group marriage. As much as extramarital sex is disapproved by those who consider it adultery, it is valued by those who favor open marriages or intimate networking.

"Infidelity" implies a violation of a promise made by two partners about sexual involvement with other people. Traditionally, spouses promise sexual fidelity, and any extramarital affair is a breach of this promise. But some couples, assuming that vows of sexual exclusivity cannot always be kept, promise to *try* to be faithful, and at the same time agree to be honest about any extramarital involvement. Whether the agreement focuses on sexual behavior, honesty, or merely not falling in love with another person, "infidelity" means breaking a promise both partners made and accepted in good faith.

You and your partner need to agree on your own meaning of infidelity so you can know the rules that govern your marriage. We will offer suggestions to help you reach your own definition, but in this chapter, we will use "infidelity" to refer to any extramarital sex.

The decisions we make about sex are never entirely personal; they are always influenced by social values. And because social values are changing today, sexual guidelines have also been changing. For a time, sexual permissiveness was thought to be increasing. On closer examination, however, it seems that the change in sexual attitudes applies only to the unmarried. Sexual experimentation before marriage is more readily accepted, but after marriage, traditional expectations prevail.

One recent survey of college students showed that not only do most *dis*approve of extramarital sex, but many even disapprove of emotional attachments with anyone other than a spouse. The importance of sexual exclusivity was also expressed by 75 percent of the men and 84 percent of the women in a nationwide survey of American couples. Most husbands and wives strongly disapprove of extramarital affairs, believing they are never justifiable.

If we were consistent with our values, the vast majority of modern American marriages would be sexually exclusive. In fact, quite a few are not. There has been surprisingly little change in the rates of extramarital sex reported during almost four decades. About one-fourth of all spouses reported having had at least one affair.

Husbands are somewhat more likely to have affairs than wives, and when they are unfaithful, it's usually with several short-term partners. Wives who are unfaithful have fewer partners, and the affairs are usually long-term. This is consistent with the general finding that men describe their affairs in sexual terms while women use emotional terms.

Nearly everyone disapproves of extramarital sex, but someone in one of every four or five houses on the block will have at least one affair. And these extramarital sexual experiences seldom stay secret for long. Some spouses are inept at deception, others deliberately leave clues, and some openly confess.

There are many reasons for revealing an affair. Some spouses can't live with the guilt, and they need the relief of a confession. Others want to express frustration about the marriage and hostility toward the spouse who "drove" them to extramarital sex. Some expose the truth so they can end the affair. And some tell all as a first step to ending the marriage.

The reasons for starting affairs are as varied as the reasons for disclosing them. We can better prevent extramarital sex from destroying our second marriages if we understand some of the reasons why people have affairs in the first place.

All of us are attracted to novelty. We enjoy our comfortable routines, like wearing old washed-out jeans and watching the same TV newscaster every night, but too much continuity can be oppressive. When we're bored, we tend to look for variety. The search for some mild excitement is one of the inescapable facts of human experience.

We vary in the ways we add spice to our lives. Some people find stimulation in relationships, whether old or new, sexual or platonic. Others seek it in work or recreation. Our search for novelty may lead us to talk to strangers, visit other countries, move to a new city, or take on new challenges at work. People who are the highest seekers of novel sensation also tend to be very sexually responsive, and they are the ones most likely to seek stimulation in sexual experiences with many partners.

The quest for sexual novelty is generally stronger in men than in women, a phenomenon once termed the "Coolidge effect". The late President and his wife are said to have taken a tour of a South Dakota poultry farm. The First Lady wistfully called the President's attention to the fact that the roosters mounted the hens with apparent enthusiasm and vigor. The President responded by pointing out how many hens were needed to stimulate this level of interest. This story captures the essence of the repeated finding that males often seek sexual variety to maintain their level of sexual desire.

We can only guess why men are more likely than women to pursue sexual novelty. Some believe it to be the result of biological evolution, while others attribute it to cultural forces. Whatever the explanation, in the vast majority of the world's cultures, men are free to pursue varied sexual partners while women are constrained to have sex only with their husbands. Understanding the causes and appreciating the universality of the practice, however, does nothing to mitigate its impact upon marriage.

The longer two people are married, the greater the allure of extramarital sex. This is usually seen as the result of boredom, which can grow as spouses become more familiar with each other. It was observed that "the history of a love affair is the drama of its fight against time," and that "familiarity dulls the edge of lust." Jessie Bernard, whose efforts to achieve equality for women are well recognized, believed that: "we will have to choose . . . . If we insist on permanence, exclusivity is harder to enforce; if we insist on exclusivity, permanence may be endangered."

These observations could make even the happiest married couple nervous, and couples whose first marriages were eroded by boredom have good reason for their anxiety. But we can control our experiences; we can choose to remain interested in each other or we can choose to give in to boredom. Boredom is not an essential byproduct of a couple's years together. If we choose to make it happen, we can learn to make our shared lives progressively more interesting as the years pass. Interest can grow as each person learns to understand the other's perspective, and as we create a shared view of life that is richer than the one either could possibly achieve alone.

Boredom occurs when we fail to give our marriage all that it deserves. We often make the mistake of taking our marriages for granted, directing our energies to work, children, self-development . . . almost anything but our spouse.

Within the first year of marriage, most spouses treat each other with less courtesy, respect, and affection than they showed in courtship. Spouses criticize each other more and praise each other less than they do total strangers. Just think about your own observations. In restaurants or at parties, if you see one couple smiling and talking together and another arguing or simply coexisting in indifferent silence, which would you guess is the married couple? The sad fact that we may receive more kindness and interest from strangers than from our spouses is one explanation for the tendency of men and women to have affairs.

We all evaluate our experience, including our marriages. Sometimes we compare current satisfactions with the joys we learned to expect from courtship or past relationships. Marriages are *satisfying* when our current happiness comes close to meeting expectations based on past experience. We may also compare the satisfactions in our marriage with those we think we might find if we lived alone or with a different partner. Marriages are *stable* when we are convinced that we are better off staying where we are than leaving for greener pastures. We all occasionally evaluate our marital satisfaction, and when the finding is "not so hot," we may wonder whether we have any better options.

Let's look at the example of Laura. Because she was unhappy with her dating experiences and her first marriage, she decided that most men are selfish and dull. When her first marriage ended, she was more relieved than disappointed. However, she began to change her mind about men when she met Jerry. He had a goal in life, and was both affectionate and considerate. As they continued to see each other, Laura decided that marriage was worth another try.

After a few years of marriage, Laura began to wonder if she had misjudged again. Jerry, who now sold commercial real estate, spent much more time uncovering properties at a steal than discovering her inner thoughts and feelings. He worked long hours, and she began to feel neglected. At this point, Laura's marriage was unhappy, but it was not yet unstable.

Laura was ready to be attracted to Chuck when she met him at an out-of-town conference. After meetings, he spent his time talking with her, and rather than discussing business, he wanted to learn more about her. As their relationship developed, he gave up golf games and football tickets to be with her. It was clear that Laura came first on Chuck's list, and she believed she had a better alternative to her second husband. At that point, her marriage become unstable.

This kind of triangle is to be expected when spouses mistreat or neglect each other over time. When a spouse feels unloved or unappreciated, the temptation to look for acceptance outside the marriage is almost universal. Before acting on this urge, we usually try to make things better at home. And even when our efforts fail, we may not enter into an affair. More than a few work or community projects (and overprotected children) are fueled by energy that's stifled in the marriage. But many people eventually do seek an outside person who will provide the affection and appreciation no longer available at home.

Some writers extol the virtues of extramarital sex. They believe it leads to increased freedom, greater sexual desire, and even renewed interest in marriage. Some couples living in sexually open marriages report that they enjoy increased equality and respect for each other as individuals, deeper companionship, and an opportunity to develop new facets of their personalities.

Despite these claims, the effect of extramarital sex on most marriages is usually negative. Ten of the 17 couples in one study of open marriage reported that their extramarital behavior caused problems including jealousy, time sharing difficulties, guilt, and resentment of the importance of the outside partner(s). The fact that spouses agree to open marriages does not protect them from its ill effects. Partners in relationships with others have less emotional and sexual energy for one another. As one partner brings less to the marriage, the other is likely to follow suit, and eventually there is little if any substance. Since intimate relationships depend on trust and closeness, they wither when these qualities disappear.

Partners who feel betrayed by their spouses will always react. Some will try to retaliate or defend themselves by taking lovers of their own. (Of course, relationships begun for revenge or self-protection are usually doomed to fail.) Others may decide not to trust anyone, and they try to avoid all relationships. Still others react by developing a physical or emotional illness. For example, one husband with a childhood history of asthma began to have severe attacks when he discovered that his wife was having an affair, forcing her to spend most of her time at his side. And another man who believed his wife was unfaithful when he was on business trips developed a fear of flying that nearly caused him to lose his job.

Most people believe that infidelity leads to divorce, and one study after another confirms this expectation. Few marriages can withstand the pressures imposed by outside sexual involvements. Fortunately, there are many ways to make fidelity a preferable and enjoyable alternative to extramarital sex.

Minimizing the Likelihood
of Extramarital Sex

The possibility of infidelity is seldom discussed in court-ship, except as it applies to the courting situation. Expectations for marital fidelity are usually part of the secret contract that is not recognized until someone breaches the "promise" he or she was probably unaware of making.

We often avoid explicit discussion of sexual expectations because the topic makes us uncomfortable. Just as many people avoid writing wills because they are afraid that the mention of death will make it happen, we may not want to consider the possibility of infidelity, especially while our marriages are still new.

Yet open discussion of the terms of the moral agreement is crucial. Because spouses often have different definitions of fidelity, one can end up being unfaithful in the eyes of the other even when there was no intention to break a promise. For example, flirtatious behavior that might be considered innocuous by one spouse could be a major threat to the other.

Remarried couples are particularly vulnerable to these misunderstandings. Those whose former spouses were unfaithful are especially sensitive to the earliest hints of infidelity in a second partner's behavior. And those who marry someone who was unfaithful to a former spouse are also especially alert for signs of a repeat of extramarital sexual activity.

As with standards of honesty, we often want to hold our partners to a higher standard of fidelity than we believe we need to follow. It may be harmless for us to show affection or flirt because we know we intend to remain faithful. But since we can not be as sure of our spouse's intentions, we often prefer that he or she have no contact with anyone we consider to be a threat.

If we wait until "innocent" behaviors provoke suspicions of infidelity, the discussion that follows is likely to be too hostile to be constructive. We can prevent many problems by reaching agreement about rules concerning infidelity before questionable behaviors confound the issue.

The following form can be used to structure your discussion of the terms of fidelity in your marriage. As always, it's best to begin by answering the questions separately.

DEFINING FIDELITY

For each of the following situations, describe the conditions under which these behaviors would and would not be acceptable. Describe the desired and undesired behaviors as they apply to both you and your spouse. Be specific about *who* is and isn't acceptable and *what* behavior is and isn't permissible.

Having lunch with friend(s) of the opposite sex

Spending evenings with friend(s) of the same sex

Spending evenings with friend(s) of the opposite sex

Taking separate vacations

Spending time with an ex-spouse or ex-lover

Flirting

Showing physical affection to a friend of the opposite sex

Having sexual intercourse with someone other than spouse

Other

After you and your partner have individually stated your preferences, compare your responses. Any time responses are the same, write the details on another sheet of paper as part of a formal agreement. When responses are different, you should negotiate until mutual agreement is reached. The following guidelines may be used to analyze and resolve differences:

1. Are the expressed desires balanced and fair? Do freedoms or restrictions apply only to one spouse? As mentioned already, most of us would like to grant ourselves more free-

dom than we give our spouse—for selfish reasons and because we trust ourselves more than we trust anyone else. The best route to a good agreement is to request only what we are willing to give.

2. When there is disagreement about the acceptability of certain behavior, explore the feelings behind one partner's desire and the other partner's fear. Then try to find an equitable compromise.

Let's say that a wife thinks the occasional separate vacation is not only acceptable but desirable, and her husband considers separate vacations an invitation to infidelity. First, each spouse should try to understand the other's point of view. Discuss feelings, not just reasons. Once both spouses understand the feelings behind the beliefs, compromise is easier. It may be that the wife only wants to visit old friends without subjecting her husband to conversations she feels would bore him. But the husband may have images of resorts offering open sex for singles. This couple could easily agree on certain kinds of separate vacations, while specifying others as off-limits.

3. When discussion fails to lead to compromise, consider temporarily accepting the more restrictive guideline, with an option to re-evaluate the agreement in six months or a year. During the early stages of second marriage, one or both partners may be smarting from past hurts, and overly vigilant about protecting the new marriage from outside threats. Once trust has developed, partners are usually willing to ease the rules.

When you reach an agreement on details, record it in writing. As with every contract, renegotiation may be necessary if circumstances or attitudes change. But after you've reached consensus, and you both clearly understand your "moral agreement," arguments or suspicions about infidelity are unlikely to occur unless someone deliberately violates the agreement.

We can make things easy or difficult for ourselves when it

comes to avoiding extramarital sex. If we've decided that
faithful is what we ought to be, we should be serious about
that commitment long before we are faced with strong temptations. "Accidental" or unplanned affairs can happen, but
only when spouses deliberately ignore the early signs of a
potential involvement.

All of us like to be reminded that we're desirable, and
when someone indicates interest, it's tempting to "play
along." Flirtations with friends or strangers can provide a
form of spontaneous excitement that even the best of marriages can't duplicate. But if we allow ourselves to be enticed
by games like these, it becomes progressively more difficult
to decide when to stop.

Obviously, it's easiest to avert an affair while it's a remote
possibility rather than an immediate temptation. Therefore,
if you intend to be faithful, you are wise to create a safety
zone by resisting the small temptations before they become
large ones.

Staying faithful does not have to be a struggle. The best
way to make fidelity an easy and pleasurable choice is to
work together to make your marriage a continuous source of
satisfaction. Our final chapter will focus on ways to assure
that both husband and wife feel accepted, understood, appreciated, and loved. Couples who develop and maintain
these feelings are seldom tempted to look for extramarital
alternatives.

11
Intimacy:
The Ultimate Fulfillment

A marriage without intimacy may be friendly, formal, and even functional, but it's certainly neither exciting, enriching, nor enjoyable.

Many couples have burned-out marriages in which the spark that died is not love, but intimacy. In public they appear to be happy, but in private they talk about their marriages with resigned dissatisfaction. They often present the confusing picture of two people who want to stay married, have enough money to afford the comforts they want, and love their children; but who dread the prospect of having to spend a three-day weekend together and regard sex with each other as more of an obligation than a pleasure.

Most of these couples were much more intimate during their courtship than they were after a few years of marriage. There was a time when they felt that magical connection we all feel with someone to whom we can say anything, and still feel appreciated and accepted.

When happy couples are asked to describe marital intimacy, the responses are usually similar. They talk of intimacy in terms of what they feel, not what they do. The descriptions often include feeling respected and valued, and trusting their mates to understand and accept any personal details they are willing to share. They generally agree upon the importance of intimacy in their marriages, and most agree that a lack of intimacy at home would be the strongest motivation for them to think about extramarital sex.

But when it comes to describing the details, people come up with a wide range of behaviors. One man mentioned his wife's knowing just how to rub his eyes when he had a headache. A woman said she felt close to her husband when he filled her coffee cup without her having to ask. Another described the way her husband lovingly touched her when they were in public, and how he listened with interest when she talked to him. With few exceptions, people's descriptions of the behaviors that contribute to feelings of intimacy are quite simple. Most of what leads to this vital feeling of closeness is not the least bit difficult to achieve. Yet for many couples, intimacy in marriage seems like an elusive and perhaps unreachable goal.

Most of us long for intimacy when we don't have it, but we often fail to recognize and appreciate it when we have it. We usually achieve it effortlessly during courtship, but we have trouble recapturing it when it fades in marriage. And when that feeling of closeness begins to wane, each partner tends to believe that the other is at fault. We are likely to focus our dissatisfaction on anything but ourselves. "He just doesn't want the openness we used to have" or "Our marriage doesn't give me the support I need" are the clarion calls of the distress we feel.

Holding a partner completely responsible for a lack of closeness is a mistake, because intimacy is a quality of relationships, not individuals. It can be achieved only through a combined effort. In the best marriages, both spouses continually give and receive enough appreciation and understanding to feel valued and loved. They provide each other with support and compassion during the hard times, and they share the joy of the good times. When we feel safe enough to divulge our innermost feelings, when we have the security of unqualified acceptance, and when we're happy to give as much or more than we receive, we've achieved the joy and comfort that only an intimate relationship can bring.

Everyone who marries expects intimacy as a natural benefit of marriage, and when it doesn't grow and deepen, we're usually angry and dissatisfied. Those of us who have been divorced may recall the loss of intimacy as the beginning of the end. Or we may have never achieved intimacy with our first partner, and its absence may have hastened the end of the marriage.

If intimacy was difficult to achieve or maintain in a first marriage, it may be even more elusive the second time around. People who have never known intimacy are often confused about what it is or how to gain it. And those who enjoyed a high level of intimacy in their first marriage and then suffered the pain of divorce may be reluctant to risk that kind of closeness again.

Are the risks of intimacy worth taking? Absolutely! Its presence makes the difference between happy and unhappy marriages, and between partners who are and aren't sexually satisfied. When intimacy is lacking, trust and commitment falter, we feel isolated, and we face the risk of developing both physical and emotional illnesses.

Although we would expect intimacy to grow stronger over time, we are more likely to lose than gain it with the years. As we've stressed before, we often take our marriages for granted and devote most of our time and energy to the demands of our jobs, homes, and children. The limited time that most of us manage to spend with each other is usually devoted to the mundane details of the day. We may establish an efficient daily routine, but when communication over a period of weeks and months is superficial, we lose the feeling of closeness. We may resign ourselves to the belief that we've simply "grown apart," when actually we've become estranged through neglect.

Estrangement can also occur when our repeated attempts fail to elicit signs of caring and support from our partners. When we yearn for closeness and understanding, a continued lack of response can increase our frustration to the point where we stop trying. Of course, this only makes the situation worse, because the less we offer, the less we receive.

Although it's common for partners to complain about feeling distant from one another, some spouses suffer from too much togetherness. It's possible to overdose on intimacy, especially when married to a person who might be labeled an "intimacy junkie." Those who are hooked on intimacy can be identified by their demands for a total "oneness" with their spouses. They regard any attempt by their mates to establish areas of independent activity as a sign of rejection. A job, a friendship, or even a hobby that isn't mutual can feel like a threat. They tend to feel mistreated any time their partners don't want exactly what they want when they want it, and they may try to keep their mates isolated from anything outside of the relationship. These smothering demands for oneness are as damaging to a marriage as is the isolation of a lack of intimacy. People who feel they need an extraordinary amount of closeness usually need to develop stronger feelings of self-esteem and independence.

Most of our frustration at not achieving a satisfying level of intimacy results from misguided attempts to gain it. The more we learn about the process of nurturing intimacy, the better our chances of enjoying it in our marriages.

Men and women seem to differ in their willingness to develop close relationships. In general, women are more verbally expressive than men, perhaps because open expression of emotion is often thought to be a virtue in women and a flaw in men. Women are more likely to enjoy and even crave intimate expression, while men may feel threatened by it. "Strong and silent" men are not even expected to *have* deep emotions, much less to *display* them. As a result, women are more likely than men to complain that their marriages lack intimacy.

When men seek closeness, they often express themselves through physical contact rather than verbal expression. Many wives complain that their husbands only show affection when initiating sex. These women are left hungering for words of affection and appreciation. Their husbands, meanwhile, may resent accusations that they are not intimate, claiming that they get no recognition for their physical expressions of affection. They usually put much more emphasis on actions than on words, and they are likely to complain that their wives are all talk and no action.

In her book *The Sex Game,* Jessie Bernard emphasizes the importance of words to women. Women are often sexually and emotionally stimulated by romantic talk that seems irrelevant to men. Men may deliver words of love in courtship, but "it is a major complaint of women that their husbands, once the honeymoon is over, rarely make verbal love to them. They scarcely even talk to them at all, let alone talk of love." Observations like these have led to the generalization that men use words to get sex, while women use sex to get words.

Of course, these are only generalizations, and many individuals vary from the norm. The problem is not that men and women have irreconcilable differences, but that we often make the false assumption that our partners want the same things we do. Even if we are aware of differences, we generally assume that our way is the right way.

A couple we saw in therapy provided a good example of how these false assumptions can cause problems. Phil and Chris sought counseling because Chris felt that her attempts to develop intimacy in the marriage had been totally unsuccessful. She was so frustrated that she was considering giving up on the marriage. Phil was also at the end of his rope; he knew that the marriage wasn't working for either one of them, but he had no idea how to make it better. Because both

Chris and Phil had difficulty describing what they wanted, they were asked to role play the kind of exchange that led to their frustrating communication. They chose to focus on responses each would want from the other after being fired from a job. This is an excerpt of what followed:

CHRIS: Phil, you must feel awful. Do you want to talk about it?

PHIL: Damn it Chris, of course I feel awful! Talking about how I feel isn't going to change anything.

CHRIS: What do you want me to do?

PHIL: I don't know, but it won't do any good to sit around feeling bad.

THERAPIST: O.K. Phil, now you respond to Chris in the same crisis.

PHIL: (putting his arm around Chris) That's tough, Chris. Have you thought about where you might find another job?

CHRIS: I don't even want to think about that now! Why can't you understand how I feel?

This exchange made their frustrations easily understandable. Chris wanted "feeling talk" when she was in crisis, so that's what she offered Phil. But Phil preferred physical affection and "action talk," and offered that to his wife. Each cared about the other, but both tried to help in exactly the wrong way. Instead of giving what the other wanted, each offered only what he or she wished to receive. The Golden Rule advises us to treat others as we would like to be treated; but when it comes to showing that we care, we are better advised to treat others as *they* would like to be treated.

The experience of Phil and Chris illustrates another important point: we often allow our partner's intimate gestures to go unnoticed because they don't fit with our definition of intimacy. Chris complained that Phil never showed any signs of caring or appreciation. In fact, it was obvious to us that he demonstrated his affection for her in a variety of ways. He looked at her lovingly, he protected and defended her when he thought she was being criticized by others, and he often put his arm around her or touched her hand. But Chris didn't think these acts were significant, because she was only interested in a certain type of self-revealing disclosure that he seldom offered. Instead of recognizing that Phil had his own way of expressing his love for her, she decided that he couldn't possibly love her because he didn't show it the way she would show it. She caused herself to suffer when she could have been enjoying a close and caring relationship.

The rewards of intimacy are mutual understanding, appreciation, and acceptance. This can be gained through a simple and direct process. First, you need to spend time together, allowing intimacy the time and space it needs to grow. Then each partner should understand what the other needs to feel valued and appreciated, so as to make it easier to deliver what's most important. It also helps to identify some goals and shared projects, to strengthen the sense of continuity that helps put some of the minor hassles in perspective. And finally, you have to take the risk of revealing your own thoughts and feelings, at the same time opening yourselves to the ideas and emotions your spouse shares with you. Taking risks and building trust create the closeness so necessary for a good marriage.

Time Together

It's no coincidence that happily married couples spend far more time together than those who are unhappy. It's obvious that we spend more time with people we like, but we also grow to like the people with whom we spend more time.

No one can say how much time is enough time. Ideally, most of us would like some time each day to talk about whatever is happening. And some time each week for shared relaxation and entertainment keeps the marriage from being overcome by routine demands. Finally, we need special times when we can communicate our deeper thoughts, feelings, and concerns.

With the pressures of daily routines, modern couples may

even need to schedule their time together. More than a few
partners have had to make "dates" with each other in order
to keep intimacy in their marriage. When children or career
responsibilities make it almost impossible to find "quality"
shared time, it's particularly important to make the most of
the time you have. Most happy couples spend a few minutes
with the children as soon as everyone comes home for dinner,
but then they spend a few minutes alone to recap the day's
events. And a few times a week, they try to find a block of
time which they can devote to sharing and understanding
each other's thoughts and feelings.

Caring and Appreciation

The next step in building intimacy is finding ways to add
meaning to time spent together. We all want to feel loved and
appreciated, and we can create loving feelings by showing
each other that we care. Of course we change from day to
day in the amount of intimacy we have and want, but to keep
our marriages strong, we should offer each other a reasonably high and consistent level of affection and appreciation.
Caring doesn't have to be expressed in a grand or costly
manner, but it should be personal and frequent. Feelings of
closeness are determined by the frequency and variety of the
ways we show we care.

We can't instinctively know what makes our partners
happy, nor can we expect that they will always know how
to please us without having to ask. If we are naive enough
to equate mindreading with love, we'll feel unloved every
time we have to ask for what we want. It makes more sense
to learn to tune in to our partners' desires by listening to
what they request, and to observe their reactions to see which
of our behaviors please and displease them.

Direct requests like "I'd like you to jog with me in the
morning" are quite clear, but observations of nonverbal behavior need to be checked out verbally, since our interpretations of nonverbal behavior aren't always correct. Every time

we think we spot our partner's wishes, it's a good idea to ask to be sure we've understood. For example, much of what we learn about our partner's sexual desires is picked up by being attentive to the way he or she responds, but it's wise to verify our impressions in words before delivering the same sexual style for the next twenty years.

Because no two people want exactly the same mix of affectionate acts, we all have to identify and fully understand our partner's desires. People in second marriages sometimes make the mistake of assuming that what pleased the first spouse will be equally pleasing to the second. But while your first spouse may have loved to have company while jogging, your second spouse may resent having you slow the pace. While your first spouse liked having company in the kitchen, your new partner may value cooking time as an opportunity to relax and be alone. And while your first partner may have liked to sleep unencumbered in the corner of a king size bed, your second may be restless unless you sleep tightly intertwined on a sliver of a double bed. New partners need to ask what they can do to please each other, and never assume they know how to please based on lessons learned in past relationships.

In addition to learning our partner's desires, we should think about gestures that help us feel loved and appreciated. If we don't ask for what we want, we have absolutely no right to expect to receive it. We owe it to our spouses and to ourselves to express our desires in positive and specific terms instead of making vague complaints about what is missing. If we can't describe what we want, we certainly can't expect our partners to figure it out. If we aren't sure what we want, it helps to look at what we give. As was the case with Phil and Chris, we often deliver what we would like to receive.

Once we can specifically define what we want, we can ask for it. The form on pages 222–23 can help clarify the expressions of caring both you and your partner would like to receive. Adapted from our *Couples' Therapy Workbook,* it is as useful to happy couples as it is to those who are less than content.

In the middle column, list those acts of caring you'd like to enjoy regularly. The items can be drawn from any facet of the relationship: communication, household duties, sex, parenting, or anything else. But they must meet the following criteria:

1.   The acts must be simple. For example, "cook a meal for my sixteen closest friends" is hardly a minor request, while "make a sack lunch for me" is reasonable.

2.   The acts must be positive. "Don't criticize me" is negative, while "help me with the dishes" is positive.

3.   Finally, the acts must be specific. "Be affectionate" is vague, whereas "kiss me goodbye when you leave the house" is specific.

Write any detail on the list that either of you interprets as a sign of caring, affection, or respect. These are the building blocks of intimacy. Requests may range from "put your dirty clothes in the hamper" to "ask me how I spent the day," from "give the kids an hour of your undivided attention" to "initiate lovemaking". All items on the list have one thing in common; they allow us to feel loved. When each person expresses interest in the other's thoughts and feelings, pitches in to do a share of the tasks that the other finds burdensome, or makes time to relax together, the message of caring comes across loud and clear.

Columns on the left and right of the form are headed "She did it" and "He did it." Use the columns to show that you noticed your spouse's caring gestures. If he picked the kids up at day care as she requested, she would write the date (e.g., 4/1) opposite that item in the "He did it" column. He would write 4/3 opposite "give me a hug" or "jog with me" if she did it on that date.

Why write the dates? Because couples tend to disagree about how frequently each expresses caring and appreciation. We are often preoccupied with other concerns and we are all better at recognizing insults and rejection than caring and acceptance. Because most of us don't notice many of the positive things we receive, recording them helps us become more aware.

We are also likely to think we give our partners more recognition and appreciation than they realize. Just as asking for what we'd like protects our partners from the burden of trying to read our minds, formally acknowledging what we receive gives our partners the satisfaction of knowing that caring gestures don't go unnoticed.

All items are written in the middle column because expressions and actions valued by one person are often valued by the other as well. You should both feel free to do anything on this list, including those items only requested by one.

We call these small but thoughtful expressions "caring behaviors." In working with distressed couples, we ask each spouse to offer at least six items on the list every day. Our observations of happy couples have shown that it's not unusual for them to exchange 30 or more caring behaviors each day.

Using this form for a week or two can help you learn specific ways to make each other happier, and we suggest updating it from time to time to keep you from growing complacent. After a while, most couples start to spontaneously do things that are on the list, and keeping records is no longer necessary. But even the happiest couples find it helpful to return to the list every once in a while as a means of updating their awareness of things they can do to build greater intimacy into their marriages.

This "caring days technique" is the first stage of our therapy for distressed couples. When we introduce it, most couples are silently indulgent because they can't imagine how small things like "make the bed if you're the last one out of it" or "be sure to tell me about articles in the paper you think I'd want to read" could possibly solve their major problems. But since the motivation behind most marital behavior is the

			Caring Behaviors			
Did It Today			Requests		Did It Today	

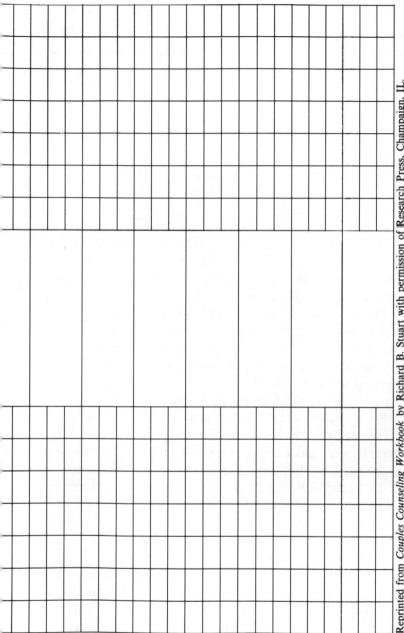

achievement of personal acceptance, these small positive behaviors are the best way for a couple to start. And it's easier to work on larger problems after both partners feel cared for and appreciated.

Sharing Goals and Interests

Daily expressions of caring are one way to keep a marriage from being dulled by tedious routine and thankless tasks. We also add quality and stability to our marriage by developing shared interests and goals.

Most of us naturally create shared concerns after we marry, often in the form of babies. When we have children, we need to work together to support them financially and emotionally. Children can provide a never-ending source of shared interest, effort, and goals.

But children are not the only foundation of mutual interest and commitment. We strengthen our marriages by saving together to buy a house or take a vacation, by participating in some of the same religious or community activities, by working together in the house or garden—in short, by sharing a wide variety of goals and interests.

Why are these shared concerns so crucial? Common goals make the daily routine more satisfying by keeping us aware that our work has some purpose. It's easier to perform some of the necessary but boring tasks if we can remind ourselves of the goals toward which we are working. It's also easier to tolerate occasional neglect from our partners when we know their efforts are directed toward mutually established goals. These goals add a continuity to our lives that allows us to keep some of our petty concerns in perspective.

Common interests keep us from becoming estranged over time. When we can spend enjoyable time with our partner and when we have a wide variety of mutually interesting topics of conversation, it's easier to stay close and involved. Although some separate interests add spice and variety to a relationship, we all need enough overlap to insure that we can enjoy discussions and activities with our partners.

Finally, shared projects and goals are a sign of commitment to the relationship. Every contribution of time, money, or effort that benefits both partners is an investment in a shared future. This future-oriented perspective helps us develop some of the security most of us hope for as a benefit of marriage.

You may want to take a few minutes to discuss and list your common goals and interests. Also list your personal goals, and discuss ways in which you can help each other achieve them. Sometimes individual fulfillment can be a couple goal as well. Finally, add any other items that you both think would add greater interest or purpose to your lives, and that would help you work even better as a team.

Openness and Vulnerability

Of all the aspects of intimacy, openness and vulnerability often present the greatest difficulties. No one likes to feel vulnerable, and most of us will do everything we can to avoid disapproval and rejection. When we can't avoid it, we try to protect ourselves by attacking or withdrawing. These defenses help maintain our self-esteem, but they are major barriers to intimacy.

Intimate information is any disclosure that creates even a little vulnerability. A revelation about a fear, weakness, or insecurity may leave us open to criticism. Expressions of positive feelings are also risky because they may not be accepted or returned. This is especially true for verbal expressions of love, which expose deep feeling of attachment and vulnerability.

For some people, almost any personal information is too intimate to disclose, while others are comfortable telling intimate details to anyone who will listen. Most of us, however, decide what to reveal according to the trust, caring, and respect we have for the other person.

Happy couples reveal more to each other than unhappy

couples do, and they are particularly good at sharing positive feelings. Unfortunately, spouses often express fewer positive emotions because they assume that their partners don't need to be told. The classic example is the man who responds to his wife's complaint that he never tells her that he loves her by saying: "Well I married you, didn't I? And have I ever asked for a divorce?" No matter how close we are, feelings must be expressed in words as well as actions. While "actions speak louder than words" and "talk is cheap," deeds alone are never enough to say "I love you."

True intimacy requires the sharing of a wide range of feelings, not just positive ones. We can only draw close to our partners by learning about them and helping them understand us. Still, as we've mentioned before, there are times when it's better not to tell all.

It's wise to withhold information that can only do harm. Revealing nostalgic memories of an old lover, or dissatisfaction with things our partners can't change are more likely to create distance than closeness. Imagine being told that your spouse thinks you're a much better person, but not nearly as exciting a lover as the one who preceded you. Some thoughts and feelings just shouldn't be shared. Since you can't know without asking, you should tell each other the kind of news you'd rather not hear.

Dr. Carl Rogers is quoted as having said: ". . . Any persistent feeling had better be expressed. Suppressing it can only . . . poison the relationship." The key word here is "persistent." When negative feelings are expressed, they should not be passing irritations. When you're annoyed at a lack of consideration, decide whether it's really worth mentioning. If it's a relatively rare event, the costs of discussing it may outweigh the benefits. But if the feeling persists, it's worthy of discussion.

Finally, any sharing of negative feelings about each other, no matter how trivial, must be discussed in a way that avoids conflict. Once an argument starts, we are too busy attacking and defending to be able to understand our partner's point of view. Since intimacy comes from acceptance and understanding, dirty fighting may be the most formidable barrier to intimacy.

It is not enough for us to offer openness and vulnerability to our partners. We must also encourage them by accepting what they choose to tell us and trying to understand rather than judge. The first step is to listen. In her book *Yes, Married: A Saga of Love and Complaint,* Judith Viorst observed: "Not listening is probably the commonest unkindness of married life, and one that creates—more devastatingly than an eternity of forgotten birthdays and misguided Christmas gifts—an atmosphere of not loving." She goes on to describe a wife's reaction to the realization that her husband has ignored her: "He isn't interested, which means I'm not interesting, which means I'm unlovable, which means I'm unloved." What begins as an attempt to move closer can become the cause of greater separation in a sad case of intimacy gone awry.

When listening to our partners' statements about feelings, we need to use everything we know about good communication. That means asking questions and checking our assumptions so we can be sure that what was heard was what was said. In addition, whether or not we agree with the feelings that are expressed, we should respond with respectful understanding.

Whenever we reveal deeper feelings, we are taking a risk. If we feel punished for our disclosures, we'll withdraw. For example, we know a woman who traces the beginning of the end of her marriage to a hurt she will never forget. She and her husband were traveling to visit her parents. They had a lot of time to talk, and as she got closer to her hometown, she revealed her fears that her parents would always treat her as an irresponsible child and never as a competent adult. Like so many people, she sometimes felt overwhelmed and confused by a mixture of guilt and love, and she was trying to describe these feelings of confusion. Her husband responded by telling her that her feelings were childish, and that she was making a big deal out of nothing. She felt so punished and demeaned for revealing her emotions that she made the decision to never again share anything important with him. As she withdrew, he followed suit, and eventually they decided they could no longer live together.

Had either one of them responded differently to the initial incident, they could have increased rather than eroded their intimacy. Her feelings deserved acceptance and he should never have put her down for revealing them. Instead of telling her that her feelings were inappropriate, he could have built intimacy by asking questions to help him understand why she felt the way she did.

She, too, could have changed the course of events. When she felt hurt, she could have explained to her husband how his response made her feel, and she could have helped him learn to improve the way he talked with her.

We are often unaware of the things we do to block intimacy. If you are in a relationship that doesn't offer enough intimacy, it's worth asking each other the following questions:

1. Am I open with you in discussing my thoughts and feelings?
2. Do I regularly ask you about your thoughts and feelings?
3. Do I express interest in the things you reveal to me?
4. Do I ever judge your feelings as unreasonable, unacceptable, or just wrong?
5. Do I ever take advantage of your self disclosures?
6. What can *I* do to help bring the two of us closer together?

Honest answers to these questions can help each of you to make it easier for the other to develop the trust, openness, respect, and appreciation that are the core of intimacy.

No relationship is effortless. We all know that. Yet most of us naively believe that when we marry, even for the second time, we are agreeing to give a little and get a lot. Unfortunately, any marriage—whether first, second, or third—won't last long if either partner begins to think that the other is taking without giving in return.

Sharing life with another person demands a series of compromises that may seem endless. He may like to fall asleep with the radio on, she with the radio off; she may like to go out for dinner, while he prefers eating at home; she may enjoy lying in bed with a good book, while he enjoys watching football games. Trouble brews when each expects the other to do things his or her way, or when compromise begins to seem like loss of faith. Marriages succeed when couples make these compromises smoothly: they fail when compromises are made reluctantly.

If spouses keep score of concessions and resent the extent to which they are asked to manage their lives in ways not strictly of their own choosing, they will battle over everything and feel satisfied with nothing. A spouse who "gives in" too much may silently tally up the sacrifices and insist on compensation for each capitulation to the partner. A more combative spouse may view each difference of opinion as a test of love or power, arguing about every minor difference. Whether conflicts are openly expressed or sullenly suppressed, couples who focus attention on the concessions they make, rather than on the compromises going their way, are doomed to be unhappy.

In a good relationship, both partners are willing to make daily concessions and to recognize the compromises their spouses have made. In the happiest marriages, partners are willing to give *before* they receive. They also work to find solutions to their problems rather than trying to justify repetition of the same mistakes. In short, we can enjoy love only if we give love.

Many first marriages fail because partners expect too much. Each professes a willingness for give-and-take, but the desire to *take* overshadows the willingness to give. As a result, neither partner gives enough, both feel punished or exploited and one or the other—or both—may eventually opt for independence.

We've tried to show that being asked to give is an *opportunity:* the more things we do to please our partners the more we can legitimately ask of them in return. Those who succeed in second marriages don't look for free rides to paradise but instead accept the importance of achieving a happy marriage "the old fashioned way—by earning it." They realize that, despite inevitable compromises, sharing life with a partner offers benefits far greater than the satisfactions available in a life alone. So they're willing to invest the energies it takes to do it right.

There's no question that even our best efforts are put to a severe test in a second marriage. Dealing with stepchildren and ex-spouses, complex finances, the demands of two careers, and the need to meld two distinctive ways of doing things can create stresses that challenge the best of relationships. And almost every person who marries for the second time occasionally makes the mistake of reacting to present problems as though they were past ones. But in the context of a loving, mutually supportive relationship the complexities of second marriage become opportunities to achieve greater intimacy, maturity, and joy.

Notes

Page 139, "around 40 percent": Section of Family Law, American Bar Association. Cited in *Family Life Educator* 2(1984):24; R. S. Weiss, "The impact of marital dissolution on income and consumption in singleparent households," *Journal of Marriage and the Family* 46(1984):115–25.

Page 142, "full-time outside jobs": P. Blumstein & P. Schwartz, *American Couples* (New York: Morrow, 1983):145. Many of the facts cited in this chapter, and not attributed to others, are based on this comprehensive study.

Page 142, "traditional division of responsibilities": S. Yogev, "Do professional women have egalitarian marital relationships?" *Journal of Marriage and the Family* 43(1981):865–71.

Page 143, "worker role": P. Freudinger, "Life satisfaction among three categories of married women," *Journal of Marriage and the Family* 45(1983):213–219.

Page 143, "regardless of competence": S. J. Bahr, "Role competence, role norms, and marital control," in *Role Structure and Analysis of the Family,* ed. F. I. Nye (Beverly Hills, CA: Sage Publications, 1976).

Page 143, "washing clothes": E. Maret & B. Finlay, "The distribution of household labor among women in dual-earner families," *Journal of Marriage and the Family* 46(1984):357–64.

Page 143, "no obligation at home": Francine S. Hall, & Douglas T. Hall, *The Two-Career Couple* (Reading, MA: Addison-Wesley, 1979), p. 114.

Page 145, "believe they should not": Blumstein and Schwartz, *American Couples,* p. 118.

Page 145, "how the children are being raised": Ibid.

Page 146, "maintaining their homes"; Lou Harris and Associates, *The General Mills American Family Report: 1980–81* (Minneapolis, MN: General Mills, 1981).

Page 151, "throughout his adult life": S. Osherson, & D. Dill, "Varying work and family choices: Their impact on men's work satisfaction," *Journal of Marriage and the Family* 45(1983):339–46.

Page 151, "occupational success": N. D. Glenn, "The contribution of marriage to the psychological well-being of males and females," *Journal of Marriage and the Family,* 37(1975):594–601.

Page 151, "including their wives": Wives are more likely to appreciate the impact of their husbands' higher earnings on their families' standard of living than to derive any vicarious satisfaction from their husbands' vocational success. A. S. Mache, G. W. Bohrnstedt & I. N. Bernstein, "Housewives' self-esteem and their husbands' success: The myth of vicarious involvement," *Journal of Marriage and the Family* 41(1979:51–7.

Page 165, "fourth marriages as well": L. L. Bumpass, "Children and marital disruption: A replication and update," *Demography* 21(1984):- 71–81.

Page 167, "children are at home": J. Belsky, G. B. Spanier, & M. Rovine, "Stability and change in marriage across the transition to parenthood," *Journal of Marriage and the Family* 45(1983):567–577; N. D. Glenn, & S. McLanahan, "Children and marital happiness: A further specification of the relationship," *Journal of Marriage and the Family* 44(1982):63–72; M. M. Marini, "Effects of the number and spacing of children on marital and parental satisfaction," *Demography* 17(1980):225–242; A. Thornton, "Children and marital stability," *Journal of Marriage and the Family* 39(1977):531–40.

Page 170, "adjustment": M. J. Bane, "Marital disruption and the lives of children," *Journal of Social Issues* 32(1976):103–17; A. Booth, D. B. Brinkerhoff, & L. K. White, "The impact of parental divorce on courtship," *Journal of Marriage and the Family* 46(1984):85–94; M. E. Lamb, "The effects of divorce on children's personality development," *Journal of Divorce* 1(1977):163–173; S. L. Nock, "Enduring effects of marital disruption and subsequent living arrangements," *Journal of Family Issues* 3(1982):25–40; H. Weingarten & R. Kulka, "Parental divorce in childhood and adult adjustment: A two-generational view" (Paper presented at the Annual Meeting of the American Psychological Association, New York, September, 1979).

Page 170, "self-concepts": S. M. Grossman, J. A. Shea & G. R. Adams, "Effects of parental divorce during early childhood on ego development and identity formation of college students," *Journal of Divorce* 3(1980):- 263–71; H. J. Raschke, & V. J. Raschke, "Family conflict and children's self-concepts: A comparison of intact and single-parent families," *Journal of Marriage and the Family* 41(1979):367–73.

Page 170, "children will themselves divorce": N. D. Glenn & B. A. Shelton, "Pre-adult background variables and divorce," *Journal of Marriage and the Family* 45(1983):405–10; E. F. Greenberg, & W. R. Nay, "The intergenerational transmission of marital instability reconsidered," *Journal of Marriage and the Family* 44(1982):335–47; H. Pope & C. W. Mueller, "The intergenerational transmission of marital instability: Comparison by race and sex," *Journal of Social Issues* 32 (1976):49–66.

Page 170, "overwhelmingly distressing experience": L. A. Kurdek, & A. E. Siesky, "Children's perceptions of their parents' divorce," *Journal of Divorce* 3(1980):339–49.

Page 170, "at each other's throats": N. Sheresky & M. Mannes, *Uncoupling—The Art of Coming Apart* (New York: Viking Press, 1972), p. 24.

Page 174, "work reasonably well":. C. R. Ahrons, "Joint custody arrangements in the postdivorce family," *Journal of Divorce* 3(1980):189–201; M. Roman, & W. Haddad, *The Disposable Parent: The Case for Joint Custody* (N.Y.: Penguin Books, 1978).

Page 208, "approach their children": R. Gilbert, A. Christensen & G. Margolin, "Patterns of alliances in nonstressed and multiproblem families," *Family Process* 23(1984):75–87; M. O. Kent, "Remarriage: A family systems perspective," *Social Casework* 61(1980):146–153.

Page 208, "how to raise children": R. B. Stuart, "Assessment and change of the communicational patterns of juvenile delinquents and their parents," in *Advances in Behavior Therapy*, ed. R. B. Rubin (New York: Academic Press, 1969), 183–197.

Page 198, "reason for divorce today": P. R. Albrecht & S. L. Kunz, "The decision to divorce: A social exchange perspective," *Journal of Divorce* 3(1980):319–37; S. P. Glass & T. L. Wright, "The relationship of extramarital sex, length of marriage, and sex differences on marital satisfaction and romanticism: Athanasiou's data reanalyzed," *Journal of Marriage and the Family* 39(1977):691–703; G. Levinger, "A social psychological perspective on marital dissolution," *Journal of Social Issues,* 32(1976):21–47; C. J. Pino, "Research and clinical application of marital autopsy in divorce counseling," *Journal of Divorce* 4(1981):31–49.

Page 200, "other than a spouse": A. P. Thompson, "Emotional and sexual components of extramarital relations," *Journal of Marriage and the Family* 46(1984):35–42.

Page 200, "American couples": P. Blumstein & P. Schwartz, *American couples* (New York: William Morrow, 1983), p. 272.

Page 200, "extramarital affairs": N. D. Glenn & N. Weaver, "Attitudes toward premarital, extramarital and homosexual relations in the U.S. in the 1970s," *Journal of Sex Research* 15(1979):108–19; A. P. Thompson, "Emotional and sexual components of extramarital relations," *Journal of Marriage and the Family* 46(1984):35–42.

Page 200, "never justifiable": Heron House Associates, *The book of numbers* (New York: A & W Publishers, 1978), p. 297.

Page 201, "four decades": Blumstein and Schwartz, *American Couples,* p. 273.

Page 201, "long term": G. B. Spanier, & R. L. Margolis, "Marital separation and extramarital sexual behavior," *Journal of Sex Research* 19(1983):23–48.

Page 201, "emotional terms": S. P. Glass & T. L. Wright, "The relationship of extramarital sex, length of marriage, and sex differences on marital satisfaction and romanticism: Athanasiou's data reanalyzed," *Journal of Marriage and the Family* 39(1977):691–7703.

Page 201, "facts of human experience": J. Jung, *Understanding Human Motivation* (New York: Macmillan, 1978), Chapter 10.

Page 202, "experiences with many partners": M. Zuckerman, *Sensation Seeking: Beyond the Optimal Level of Arousal* (Hillsdale, N.J.: Lawrence Erlbaum, 1979), pp. 271–277.

Page 202, "only with their husbands": G. P. Murdock, *Social Structure* (New York: Free Press, 1949).

Page 202, "fight against time": G. Homans, *Social Behavior: Its Elementary Forms* (New York: Harcourt, 1961), p. 203.

Page 202, "edge of lust": D. Symons, *The Evolution of Human Sexuality* (New York: Oxford University Press, 1979), p. 110.

Page 202, "permanence may be endangered": J. Bernard, "Infidelity: some moral and social issues," in *Beyond Monogamy* eds J. R. Smith & L. G. Smith, (Baltimore: Johns Hopkins University Press, 1974), p. 138.

Page 203, "total strangers": R.G. Ryder, "Husband-wife dyads versus married strangers," *Family Process* 7(1968):223–28; R.B. Stuart & J. Braver, "Positive and negative exchanges between spouses and strangers" (Paper presented at the Annual Meeting of the American Psychological Association, 1973).

Page 205, "new facets of their personalities": J. J. Knapp, *The Journal of Sex Research* 12(1976):206–19; J. W. Ramey, "Intimate groups and networks: Frequent consequence of sexually open marriage," *The Family Coordinator* 24(1975):515–30.

Page 205, "infidelity leads to divorce": M. R. Laner & S. L. Housker, "Sexual permisiveness in younger and older adults," *Journal of Family Issues* 1(1980):103–24.

Page 219, "Couple's Therapy Workbook": R.B. Stuart, *Couples' Therapy Workbook* (Champaign, IL: Research Press, 1983).

Suggested Readings

1. For an overview of the way in which contemporary couples deal with the issues of money, work, and sex, we recommend: Blumstein, Philip & Schwartz, Pepper. *American Couples.* New York: William Morrow & Co., 1983.

2. For more information about antenuptial and living-together contracts, see: Weitzman, Lenore J. *The Marriage Contract: A Guide to Living with Lovers and Spouses.* New York: The Free Press, 1981.

3. A thoughtful account of the challenges faced by two-career couples is found in: Hall, Francine S. & Hall, Douglas T. *The Two-Career Couple.* Reading, Mass.: Addison-Wesley, 1979.

4. For more information about Stepparenting, see: Visher, Emily, and Visher John. *How to Win as a Stepfamily.* New York: Dembner Books, 1982.

5. An overview of the logic of many of the techniques we describe may be of interest to professionals. See: Stuart, Richard B. *Helping Couples Change.* New York: Guilford Press, 1980.

6. An insightful and readable approach to dealing with a wide range of

stresses faced by couples is found in: Broderick, Carlfred. *Couples.* New York: Simon & Schuster, 1979.

7. The following are the best of the many books we've read on communication.

a. The philosophy of communication is elegantly described in: Watzlawick, Paul; Beavin-Bavelas, Janet; and Jackson, Don D. *Pragmatics of Human Communication.* New York: W.W. Norton, 1967.

b. Interesting observations on male-female differences in communication are found in: Bernard, Jessie. *The Sex Game: Communication Between the Sexes.* New York: Atheneum, 1975.

c. A well-documented yet highly readable text on communication is: Wilmot, William W.. *Dyadic Communication.* Reading, Mass.: Addison-Wesley, 1979.

d. Communication patterns in family interaction are well-analyzed in: Glavin, Kathleen M., & Brommel, Bernard J. *Family Communication: Cohesion and Change.* Glenview, Ill.: Scott Foresman & Co., 1982.

e. A good self-help manual on improving communication and conflict management is: Gottman, John; Notarius, Cliff; Gonso, Jonni; & Markman, Howard. *A Couple's Guide to Communication.* Champaign, Ill.: Research Press, 1976.

f. Clear and helpful guidelines for intimacy-enhancing conflict resolution are presented in: Paul, Jordan, & Paul, Margaret. *Do I Have To Give Up Me To Be Loved By You?* Minneapolis, Minn.: Compcare, 1983.

8. An audiotape demonstration of good and bad communication patterns in couples, with guidelines for building intimacy is found in: Jacobson, Barbara, & Stuart, Richard B. *Caring and Understanding: A Guide to Improving Communication.* New York: BMA/Guilford Press, 1985.

Index